Human Trafficking Hysteria

Through cultural criminology, this book brings together existing research to provide an overview of historical and modern moral panics related to human trafficking.

What do you picture when you hear the words human trafficking? Perhaps you imagine someone kidnapped and sold as shown in films or worry that sex trafficking increasingly occurs online or in big cities during major events. While sex trafficking does occur, the reality of human trafficking is complex, though this reality is often obscured by the media. The media has played a large role in shaping understanding of this crime, with panics, conspiracies, and misinformation abounding. This book uses cultural criminology to break down historical and modern panics to understand the links between media portrayals of human trafficking, perpetuation of stereotypes, and influences on policy. The text examines the impacts of human trafficking panics perpetuated by media, including understanding the origins of human trafficking in the nineteenth-century White slave panic, the ways that popular media perpetuates stereotypes, the reality of trafficking at sporting events, and the role of social media in generating misinformation.

Human Trafficking Hysteria is a valuable resource for criminology and sociology classes, as well as special-topics classes on sex crimes, victimization, or the media.

Sarah Hupp Williamson is an Associate Professor of Criminology at the University of West Georgia. Her several lines of research examine the intersections of globalization, inequality, and crime. She is the author of Human Trafficking in the Era of Global Migration: Unraveling the Impact of Neoliberal Economic Policy and Criminology Explains Human Trafficking.

Routledge Studies in Crime, Culture and Media

Routledge Studies in Crime, Culture and Media offers the very best in research that seeks to understand crime through the context of culture, cultural processes and media.

The series welcomes monographs and edited volumes from across the globe, and across a variety of disciplines. Books will offer fresh insights on a range of topics, including news reporting of crime; moral panics and trial by media; media and the police; crime in film; crime in fiction; crime in TV; crime and music; 'reality' crime shows; the impact of new media including mobile, Internet and digital technologies, and social networking sites; the ways media portrayals of crime influence government policy and lawmaking; the theoretical, conceptual and methodological underpinnings of cultural criminology.

Books in the series will be essential reading for those researching and studying criminology, media studies, cultural studies and sociology.

A Popular Criminology of Youth Justice
Youth on Film
Jessica Urwin

America's Horror Stories
U.S. History Through Dark Tourism
Kevin Revier and Favian Alejandro Martín

Sexual and Physical Violence in Australian Punk and Hardcore Music Scenes
Ash Barnes

Human Trafficking Hysteria
Historical and Modern Perspectives on Moral Panics, Media, and Crime
Sarah Hupp Williamson

Human Trafficking Hysteria

Historical and Modern Perspectives on Moral Panics, Media, and Crime

Sarah Hupp Williamson

LONDON AND NEW YORK

First published 2025
by Routledge
4 Park Square, Milton Park, Abingdon, Oxon OX14 4RN

and by Routledge
605 Third Avenue, New York, NY 10158

Routledge is an imprint of the Taylor & Francis Group, an informa business

British Library Cataloguing-in-Publication Data
A catalogue record for this book is available from the British Library

Library of Congress Cataloging-in-Publication Data
Names: Williamson, Sarah Hupp, author.
Title: Human trafficking hysteria: historical and modern perspectives on moral panics, media, and crime / Sarah Hupp Williamson.
Description: Abingdon, Oxon; New York, NY: Routledge, 2025. | Series: Routledge studies in crime, culture and media | Includes bibliographical references and index.
Identifiers: LCCN 2024047824 (print) | LCCN 2024047825 (ebook) | ISBN 9781032573564 (hardback) | ISBN 9781032573571 (paperback) | ISBN 9781003439004 (ebook)
Subjects: LCSH: Human trafficking. | Moral panics. | Mass media and crime.
Classification: LCC HQ281 .W479 2025 (print) | LCC HQ281 (ebook) | DDC 362.88/51–dc23/eng/20241122
LC record available at https://lccn.loc.gov/2024047824
LC ebook record available at https://lccn.loc.gov/2024047825

ISBN: 9781032573564 (hbk)
ISBN: 9781032573571 (pbk)
ISBN: 9781003439004 (ebk)

DOI: 10.4324/9781003439004

Typeset in Times New Roman
by Deanta Global Publishing Services, Chennai, India

Contents

1 Introduction to Human Trafficking[1]

Types of Human Trafficking

Human trafficking is a complex and multifaceted phenomenon, though there are several myths that persist about it. One prominent myth is that human trafficking only occurs for sexual exploitation (Stickle et al., 2020). While sex trafficking does occur, human trafficking takes many forms. Definitions of human trafficking have come to include not only sexual exploitation but also practices around labor exploitation, organ trafficking, forced marriage, child soldiers, and debt bondage. Women and children have often been the focus of anti-trafficking efforts, but the reality is that trafficking affects persons of all races, ages, gender, sexuality, or nationality (Stickle et al., 2020).

Human trafficking also does not have to involve travel across state or national borders or movement of any kind (Kakar, 2017). In fact, someone may be trafficked in their own hometown. While international trafficking has been placed high on the agenda of governments around the world, internal or domestic trafficking may be a greater problem for most countries (Aronowitz, 2009). Human trafficking is often thought of as a crime occurring in seedy, underground places, but it frequently occurs in legal industries (Kakar, 2017). While things like brothels and red-light districts may come to mind when thinking about the issue, human trafficking happens in work such as agriculture, restaurants, and domestic work. Finally, unlike frequent media depictions, human trafficking does not have to involve physical force or bondage (Stickle et al., 2020). There are many ways in which traffickers may exert control over victims, and physical violence is just one. Other common tactics of control include psychological abuse, threats, and fraud or deception (CTDC, 2021). Throughout this book, various moral panics around human trafficking will be explored, providing an understanding of where some of these stereotypes have emerged from and how they continue to shape current perceptions, responses, and policies around human trafficking.

To begin, however, the two primary types of human trafficking are briefly outlined. This includes sex trafficking and labor trafficking. While there are many other forms of trafficking, including things like child soldiers, trafficking

DOI: 10.4324/9781003439004-1

in persons for organ removal, and trafficking for forced criminality, sex and labor make up the majority of trafficking victimizations.

Sex Trafficking

The media is biased toward reporting on sex trafficking more frequently than other forms of trafficking, often focusing on women and children. Because of this, the general public is often more aware of sex trafficking than other types (Stickle et al., 2020). Sex trafficking is a broad category that includes a variety of sexual acts performed under force, fraud, or coercion. Under the US federal definition as well as the UN definition, if the individual performing the acts is under 18, force, fraud, or coercion are not required to define the act as sex trafficking (Stickle et al., 2020). These acts may occur in strip clubs, hotels, truck stops, during private parties, and more (Nichols, 2016).

Acts included under the umbrella of sex trafficking may include escort services, outdoor solicitation, pornography, personal sexual servitude, and brothels (Polaris, 2017). Outdoor solicitation occurs when trafficking victims are forced to seek out buyers in an outdoor setting, often in a particular area of a city or at a select location such as a truck stop. A study of the street commercial sex industry in NYC shows that women and girls of color are disproportionately represented in the data (Polaris, 2017). Escort services occur when trafficking victims go to a buyer's hotel, residence, or party, with advertising on the internet often facilitating the job. These victims may be deceived by having been promised a false job, such as a modeling contract (Polaris, 2017). Remote interactive sexual acts are a category that includes webcamming, text-based chats, and phone sex lines (Polaris, 2017).

The use of kidnapping or abduction in sex trafficking does occur, though it is rare. More frequently, entry into sex trafficking involves boyfriend pimps, family traffickers, peer influences, and survival sex (exchanging sex to meet immediate needs such as food and shelter). Pimps may target vulnerable individuals, forming a romantic relationship with them first, then facilitating their involvement in commercial sex (Nichols, 2016). Some of the vulnerabilities linked to sex trafficking include poverty, homelessness, involvement in the child welfare system, a history of trauma and abuse, and addiction (Stickle et al., 2020).

Many factors may prevent a victim from leaving their trafficking situation. These include "emotional barriers, stigmatization, abuses, debt bondage, cultural beliefs, and gaps in services" (Nichols, 2016, p. 106). Trauma-coerced attachment to their traffickers may also hinder a victim from leaving. Research shows that the defining features of trauma-coerced attachment include the use of control tactics, exploitation of power in the relationship, alternating between rewards and punishment, and victim internationalization of the trafficker's view (Casassa et al., 2022; Doychak & Raghavan, 2020; Sanchez et al., 2019). Victim vulnerabilities are exploited by the trafficker to coercively control them and develop an attachment. Victims experience manipulation, isolation, degradation, physical and sexual violence, and more. At the same time, positive behavior is displayed intermittently by the trafficker, including tangible gifts or affection and intimacy. In combination with isolation, this can alter the victim's perspective, leading to dependency on the trafficker and an adoption of the abuser's view. This trauma-coerced attachment can ultimately lead the victim to take responsibility for the abuser's crimes, protect them, and even seek to return to them (Chambers et al., 2024).

Labor Trafficking

While sex trafficking has often received more attention, resources, and funding, awareness of labor trafficking is growing. Some experts argue that labor trafficking may actually be more prevalent than sex trafficking, though it often goes unreported and undetected (Cockbain & Bowers, 2019). Local law enforcement agencies do not tend to prioritize labor trafficking and have difficulty defining and identifying situations of labor trafficking (Owens et al., 2014). Labor trafficking involves making someone perform labor or service through the use of force, fraud, or coercion (Stickle et al., 2020). As with sex trafficking, kidnapping and abduction are rare, as are victims who are physically unable to leave due to being chained up (Polaris, 2021a). Instead, traffickers use a variety of recruitment tactics such as false promises and fraud and rely on tactics such as withholding wages and documents; physical, sexual, and emotional abuse; debt bondage; and threats against themselves and family members to maintain control over victims (Owens et al., 2014; Polaris, 2021a, 2021b; Stickle et al., 2020).

The demand for cheap labor and goods contributes to the issue of labor trafficking (Stickle et al., 2020). Labor trafficking is found in a wide variety of industries that can be isolated or within the public eye, including domestic work, food and restaurant service, agriculture, construction, hospitality, landscaping, and manufacturing (Polaris, 2017). Though labor trafficking can occur with citizens, frequently foreign nationals working on a visa are at an elevated risk. The structure of a country's visa system may put workers at risk for exploitation and trafficking. In the US, temporary work visas are tied to a single employer, meaning that they cannot leave their job for another, who may also control their food and housing. In Saudi Arabia and other Gulf countries, foreign workers cannot leave the country, quit their jobs, or switch employment without permission from their current employer (Stickle et al., 2020). Employers may exploit the visa process, demanding fees and costs that are then used to coerce the victims to stay to pay off the debt and presenting contracts that take advantage of the workers' lack of English fluency and unfamiliarity with the local culture. Employers may also let visas expire and then use the threat of reporting the now unauthorized workers for deportation as a means to control them (Stickle et al., 2020).

Labor trafficking in domestic work includes a variety of services ranging from managing households, cleaning, cooking, and taking care of children, the elderly, or the ill. Factors that facilitate labor trafficking in domestic work include "poverty, weak protections for workers at the country level, cultural and linguistic isolation of workers, and physical isolation in private homes" (Stickle et al., 2020, p. 226). In the US, domestic workers are not included in many labor laws, including the National Labor Relations Act of 1935 and the Fair Labor Standards Act of 1938 (Polaris, 2019). Certain types of visas are also associated with this type of trafficking. Specifically,

> domestic workers with A-3 and G-5 visas are especially vulnerable to the imbalanced power dynamic inherent in temporary work visas due to the trafficker's elevated status as a diplomat, royal, or high-ranking member of an influential international organization. This status makes the fear of speaking out even greater and can allow traffickers to continue exploiting victims under the protection of diplomatic immunity.
>
> (Polaris, 2017, p. 21)

Labor trafficking in agriculture and animal husbandry has been reported in corn fields, orange orchards, and dairy farms, though more labor-intensive crops like tobacco may be more susceptible to trafficking (Polaris, 2017). In the US, foreign workers on H-2A visas and undocumented workers have frequently been connected to labor trafficking (Owens et al., 2014; Polaris, 2021a). One study of labor trafficking among agricultural workers on H-2A visas found that in addition to working excessive hours and having their wages withheld, 58% were threatened with immigration consequences such as deportation and 32% were threatened with being blacklisted from working in the United States again (Polaris, 2021a). Trafficking in the commercial fisheries sector has also been found, with many documented cases occurring in the Greater Mekong sub-region, and in particular, Thailand (ILO, 2013). The isolation of fishing vessels at sea for long periods of time, lack of transparency around contracts and pay, inadequate protections, and control over identity documents make fishers vulnerable to deceptive and coercive working conditions (ILO, 2013).

Research suggests that labor trafficking survivors experience similar trauma to sex trafficking survivors. A study of 66 sex trafficking and 65 labor trafficking survivors found that 71% of respondents met the diagnostic criteria for depression, and 61% met the diagnostic criteria for PTSD, with no significant differences by type of trafficking victimization (Hopper & Gonzalez, 2018). Labor trafficking victims also face similar barriers to exiting trafficking, though labor trafficking victims may be more reluctant to contact law enforcement due to fear of deportation (Owens et al., 2014).

Causes of Human Trafficking

Research on the causes of human trafficking comes from a variety of disciplines, including criminology, sociology, social work, political science, and economics. Yet the findings across these disciplines are consistent in what they have found to be recurring causes of human trafficking. There are several root factors that are connected to vulnerability to human trafficking, including globalization, economic inequality, gender inequality, racial/ethnic discrimination, conflict, and corruption. Briefly, some of the major causes of trafficking are reviewed here.

Globalization

Globalization can be defined as a set of processes that hinder or facilitate the international flows of individuals, items, and information (Ritzer, 2010). The structural and cultural changes associated with globalization have exacerbated inequalities while also creating a demand for unmet labor needs which drives migration (Lee, 2011). Structurally, the industries of local economies have been transformed under globalization as migration and trading across borders increases. There is a demand for cheap, low-skilled labor in industries like domestic work, agriculture, construction, and manufacturing—the same sectors that are also likely to experience trafficking (Aronowitz, 2017).

Unequal economic development from globalization has also created a wide gap of global inequalities between countries, and even within countries there is a widening gap between poor and rich communities (Chuang, 2006; Zhang, 2007). This gap then creates a growing population of individuals who use migration as a means to attain economic gain (Chuang, 2006; Surtees, 2008). Through globalization, it is important to consider the ways in which migration is linked with vulnerability to human trafficking, including demand for labor and increased hopes (Chuang, 2006; Shelley, 2010). By placing human trafficking within the larger global migratory movement, it becomes possible to understand how the pull of unmet labor demands across borders combined with restrictive immigration policies leads individuals to seek out alternative routes, placing them at risk of trafficking victimization (Chuang, 2006; Lee, 2011; Shelley, 2010).

In addition to structural changes, globalization and urbanization have led to massive cultural changes as the spread of global media and the internet allows for communities to receive an influx of messages that promise better chances and opportunities elsewhere (Aronowitz, 2017; Chuang, 2006). Growing structural inequalities combine with these cultural aspirations to foster an environment that encourages decisions to migrate (Cameron & Newman, 2008; Chuang, 2006; Mishra, 2015). Individuals become vulnerable to trafficking through false promises of job and educational opportunities. In this way, globalization creates a structural environment that limits the opportunities of some and a cultural environment that contributes to fostering hopes and expectations. Together, these may inform individuals' willingness to migrate, increasing their trafficking victimization risk (Cameron & Newman, 2008; Chuang, 2006).

Economic Inequality

Globalization has worsened economic inequalities and further marginalized vulnerable populations (Farr, 2004; Kara, 2010; Limoncelli, 2009a; Shelley, 2010; Stone, 2005; Truong, 2003). One way this has occurred is through economic restructuring which removes important government social safety nets (Corrin, 2005; Hupp Williamson, 2017; Kligman & Limoncelli, 2005; Surtees, 2008). Institutions like the IMF and World Bank have been instrumental in guiding economic policy in developing countries. The outcomes of such policies, however, have often had the adverse effect of worsening economic inequalities (Hupp Williamson, 2022).

Economic deprivation and insecurity can exacerbate vulnerability and make migration for work or other economic opportunities appear as a viable option (Chuang, 2006; Surtees, 2008). Risky migration decisions linked to trafficking victimization go hand-in-hand with economic-based disparities such as poverty and blocked job or educational opportunities (Bales, 2005; Cameron & Newman, 2008; Farr, 2004; Jac-Kucharski, 2012; Mishra, 2015; Outshoorn, 2015; Truong, 2003; Zhang, 2007). Traffickers can ultimately exploit these vulnerable populations by deceiving individuals with promises of jobs or education (Cameron & Newman, 2008; Hughes, 2000). Conditions of poverty not only drive trafficking flows from poor to wealthier countries, but also from rural to urban areas within countries (Aronowitz, 2017).

Gender Inequality

Gender-based inequality, including discrimination and violence, is also an important cause of human trafficking (Chuang, 2006; Corrin, 2005; Farr, 2004; Kara, 2010; Lee, 2011; Limoncelli, 2009a). Research shows that a lack of economic and social rights and opportunities—including property rights, educational access, and political participation—are important factors in the trafficking of women and girls (Shelley, 2010). Gender-based inequalities are also connected to the "feminization of poverty," where women and children are disproportionately impoverished in a population (Chuang, 2006; Corrin, 2005; Hughes, 2000; Hupp Williamson, 2017; Lee, 2011).

Under such circumstances, the concept of "feminization of survival" is used to refer to family and community reliance on women to migrate for economic sustenance (Sassen, 2002). Also referred to as "survival migrants," it is the need for work that combines with the contradictory demand for workers and tightening migration restrictions in destination countries that leave these migrants at risk of trafficking victimization. For women, these circumstances are only magnified by gender-based employment discrimination that pushes them to informal economic sectors, which lack legal migration routes (Chuang, 2006). Both the feminization of poverty and the feminization of survival demonstrate that globalization is gendered, often leading to the "feminization of irregular migration" (Lee, 2011). In short, poverty and discrimination are often compounded for women, leading them to seek ways to migrate for more prosperous opportunities (Outshoorn, 2015). Such migration leaves women vulnerable to trafficking not only during their movement but also once they have reached their destination.

Racial and Ethnic Inequality

Racial and ethnic-based discrimination, stereotypes, and cultural oppression can also contribute to an individual's vulnerability to human trafficking. Such discrimination can block equal access to income, education, housing, and legal protections, leading to marginalization (Bryant-Davis & Tummala-Narra, 2017). For example, in Latin America, indigenous populations are at risk for labor trafficking (Cameron & Newman, 2008), while ethnic minorities in Thailand and Moldova experience high rates of sex trafficking (Shelley, 2010).

Racism also intersects with, and intensifies, class- and gender-based inequalities, making it important to look at issues of poverty, gender, and race together. Too often, women of color face marginalized access to education and employment. This vulnerability is capitalized on by the sex industry, as sexist stereotypes based on race and ethnicity create a demand for women from nations in the global South and East (Bryant-Davis & Tummala-Narra, 2017; Chong, 2014; Kempadoo, 2001; Limoncelli, 2009b). Women of color may be forced or coerced into sexual labor, contributing to their overrepresentation "at the bottom, most dangerous levels" (Limoncelli, 2009b, p. 266). Ultimately, much of the research on minority victimization in human trafficking notes that it is a compounding of vulnerabilities through discrimination and marginalization in multiple areas which places them at a high risk of trafficking (Butler, 2015; Chong, 2014; Chuang, 2006; Corrin, 2005; Kara, 2010; Limoncelli, 2009a; Todres, 2009).

Conflict

Human trafficking has been documented as the direct or indirect result of armed conflict in countries such as Afghanistan, Libya, the Philippines, and Somalia (Kangaspunta et al., 2018). More specifically, conflict in the form of civil conflict, war, violent militarization, and social unrest has been implicated in creating human trafficking flows (Bales, 2004; Cameron & Newman, 2008; Lee, 2011; Mishra, 2015; Shelley, 2010). Such conflicts create social disorganization and weaken social institutions, leading to deterioration in the rule of law, community and family, and social and economic protections (Kangaspunta et al., 2018).

Along with militarization and displacement, these conditions are associated with an increase in both the supply and demand of human trafficking

(Limoncelli, 2009a). That is to say, these conditions often act to drive individuals to seek migration out of the area, placing them at risk of victimization by trafficking. As conflicts erode economic and social institutions, displaced individuals and refugees are populations vulnerable to trafficking through migration and exploitation (Akee et al., 2010). Further, studies show that measures of conflict and a high presence of displaced persons and refugees in a country are predictive of that country's likelihood of experiencing human trafficking, meaning the link between conflict and trafficking cannot be ignored (Akee et al., 2010).

Corruption

Corruption is not so much a cause of human trafficking, as it is a facilitator. Corruption acts to enable and exacerbate human trafficking. A country's level of corruption has been shown to play a role in allowing the offenders of trafficking to continue their crimes, which can erode perceptions of the legitimacy of law enforcement and the law among victims, ultimately undermining anti-trafficking policy and law enforcement within a country (Farr, 2004; Jac-Kucharski, 2012; Malarek, 2011; Surtees, 2008). Globalization has created favorable contexts for crime by facilitating corruption, including organized crime groups involvement in transnational crimes such as trafficking (Lee, 2011; Shelley, 2010). The action or inaction of law enforcement and public officials through corruption allows the traffickers to continue to exploit individuals (Malarek, 2011).

In addition to corruption being influential in traffickers' ability to evade prosecution for their crimes, the legal framework often works in their favor as well. Studies have shown that levels of compliance with anti-trafficking laws vary by country and are impacted by factors such as corruption and the rights of women (Avdeyeva, 2012; Cho et al., 2014). Research also shows that countries may be selective in their enforcement, focusing on aspects that reflect economic interests such as border control, rather than the protection of human rights or prosecution of offenders (Cho & Vadlamannati, 2012; Hacker, 2015).

Researching Human Trafficking

Researching human trafficking is often a difficult task, and gathering data on the issue presents several obstacles. First, and perhaps most influential, is the fact that the nature of the crime of human trafficking means that it generally goes undetected and undocumented (Kakar, 2017; Laczko & Gramegna, 2003). Human trafficking victims are a hidden population, a group whose size and boundaries are unknown and whose membership often falls into stigmatized or illegal categories, such as being undocumented or a sex worker (DoCarmo, 2020; Tyldum & Brunovskis, 2005). In regard to research, gaining access to trafficked individuals is extremely difficult. As a vulnerable population, service providers, attorneys, and law enforcement may resist victims participating in research to protect them from the possibility of further exploitation or adverse impacts from recounting their experiences (Goździak, 2015). These issues are only further exacerbated when working with minor victims of trafficking (Rothman et al., 2018).

Overall, there is also a lack of systematic and comparable data on the issue (Kakar, 2017). Popular writing on human trafficking tends to remain anecdotal, simple, and sensationalistic (Weitzer, 2014). Reports from government agencies and non-governmental organizations often fail to detail the sources of the numbers they report and cannot be verified (Goodey, 2008; Weitzer, 2014; Zhang, 2009). Among academic studies, the literature remains largely focused on generating estimates, describing cross-national routes of trafficking, and reviewing legal responses (Goździak, 2015). Studies have been criticized for sampling issues, poorly designed survey questions, limited scope, empirically unsupported claims, and a skewed focus toward sex trafficking (Cockbain et al., 2018; Tyldum, 2010; Zhang, 2009).

One issue contributing to the lack of comparable data is that both within the United States, and at the regional and international levels, there is no single agency that acts as a focal point for the collection of statistics on human trafficking (Bales et al., 2020; Laczko & Gramegna, 2003). Instead, different organizations collect information and research on trafficking, each through the lens and interests that are the focus of that organization and its mandate. For example, the International Organization for Migration (IOM) is likely to focus on issues related to restrictive migration policies, labor demands, and the potential for exploitation, while the United Nations Office of Drugs and Crime (UNODC) may focus on tracing international trafficking routes and the country patterns of international trafficking.

Among what data is available, definitional issues lead to problems of data validity and make comparisons difficult. Existing data is often program-specific, meaning that the data is based on the various definitions of human trafficking used by each individual agency and organization (Bales et al., 2020; Laczko & Gramegna, 2003). When there is a lack of uniformity among the various definitions of human trafficking used by governments, organizations, and researchers, estimates of the nature and extent of human trafficking will vary (Kakar, 2017). The issue of human trafficking covers a wide range of processes, actions, and outcomes. Organizations may differ in the data they collect due to this, focusing on different stages such as recruitment, transportation, or control at the final destination. Further, individuals may appear in data from multiple organizations leading to accuracy problems in estimates (Laczko & Gramegna, 2003).

In addition to variations in definitions across organizations, definitions also vary across countries. In many countries data collection, it is still common to co-mingle data on trafficking, smuggling, irregular migration, and sex workers (Doezema, 2010; Weitzer, 2014). Some countries include the transportation of a woman across a border for the purpose of prostitution in their definitions of trafficking, regardless of the consent of the woman. In other cases, migrants working in the sex trade may be subsumed under the trafficking definition regardless of their consent and conditions of labor (Chapkis, 2003; Doezema, 2010; Petrunov, 2014). Other countries may not even recognize labor trafficking in their legal codes (Savona & Stefanizzi, 2007).

The conflation of human trafficking with other issues, such as smuggling, prostitution, and even slavery creates issues with data. For example, the US government recently began equating human trafficking with slavery in its reports, with the terms trafficking and slavery being used interchangeably in the State Department's 2012 and 2013 annual reports. This change resulted in a large spike in the number of estimated victims (Weitzer, 2015). Such conflation can lead to dramatic increases in estimates of human trafficking that are not accurate reflections of the potential population.

Countries may also be resistant to cooperating with and coordinating data collection efforts at a cross-national level. Trafficking data may be regarded as classified or privacy laws may prohibit sharing what is often personal information (Laczko & Gramegna, 2003). Nations may also be unwilling to share data that they feel will reflect negatively on their government or be used against them in the form of sanctions (Feingold, 2011). The sharing of data between source and destination countries can be very beneficial but often occurs only when necessary or not at all due to concerns about authorities and agencies in the source country being involved in trafficking themselves (Laczko & Gramegna, 2003).

Data on the number of persons being trafficked are often only estimates and are generally regarded as unreliable (GAO, 2006; Goździak, 2015). National estimates of human trafficking are often extrapolated from the number of criminal cases, which represent only a small portion of identified cases. These estimates are often repeated without verification and may even be misinterpreted as actual and known numbers of human trafficking victims (Fedina, 2015; Zhang, 2009).

The Global Slavery Index (GSI) perhaps best represents these methodological issues. Started in 2013 by an NGO, the GSI ranks countries on their prevalence of slavery. The index demonstrates definitional issues before even getting to the estimates, as they define slavery to include both human trafficking, forced labor, and slavery practices (Weitzer, 2014). To create their estimates, the GSI draws on a variety of sources, ranging from news media, NGO reports, surveys, and official government agencies, each of which may work from different definitions and viewpoints, leading to noncomparable data. For the countries without this data, the GSI assigns an estimate based on the estimate from a country deemed comparable and relevant (Gallagher, 2017; Weitzer, 2014). Such a system ultimately means that the estimates presented by the GSI are inaccurate representations of human trafficking in a country.

Data on Human Trafficking Today

So where does our knowledge about human trafficking come from and what does human trafficking today looks like based on this data? There are a variety of data sources that human trafficking researchers may make use of for both quantitative and qualitative studies. Quantitative studies tend to focus on estimates, frequencies, trends, and opinions of human trafficking (Russell, 2018). Official government statistics are one data source that quantitative researchers may make use of. In the US, the FBI established Human Trafficking (UCR-HT) data collection as part of its Uniform Crime Reporting (UCR) Program in 2013. State and local law enforcement agencies that participate in this collection provide counts of offenses, case clearances, and arrests for human trafficking for the purpose of commercial sex acts or involuntary servitude. The 2019 report shows a total of 1,883 incidents of human trafficking were reported that year, with 85% reported in the category of commercial sex acts.

As with other crimes, there are several drawbacks to the use of official statistics. Data from official sources, such as criminal justice agencies, are likely to be undercounts of the true numbers of human trafficking. This is, in large part, due to law enforcement deficiencies in identifying and reporting cases of human trafficking (Farrell & Reichert, 2017). Because of this, the number of victims recorded by law enforcement may be a better indicator of the effectiveness and functionality of law enforcement in a country, rather than a good estimate of the number of human trafficking victims (Tyldum & Brunovskis, 2005). Often, however, official reports may be one of the few sources of data on identified victims available in a particular country.

Globally, organizations like the United Nations and Interpol can act as sources that bring together statistics from a variety of cross-national sources. The UNODC SHERLOC Database hosts a database of legislation on human trafficking in countries around the world, as well as a case law database. This data can be used to not only study differences and similarities in the laws in various nations but also to examine details on victims and perpetrators, verdicts, and other information from prosecuted cases of trafficking across the world. For example, cases from the 2020 UNODC Global Report on Trafficking in Persons tell us that the majority of persons investigated or arrested, prosecuted, and/or convicted of trafficking in persons are male, comprising over 60% of the total. Thirty-six percent of those prosecuted for trafficking were female and were more likely to be involved in the recruitment phase.

The UNODC has produced six of these global reports on human trafficking since 2009, with the aim to provide an overview of patterns, flows, and current issues of human trafficking around the world. Data for the 2020 report is drawn from information on the detected victims and convicted traffickers across 148 countries. Globally, victims are typically trafficked within geographically close areas, with most detected victims being citizens of the countries where they are detected. Data shows that domestic trafficking is a growing issue compared to the often-focused issue of cross-national trafficking. Sixty-five percent of trafficking cases were reported as domestic, with only 15% involving victims from another region. Domestic trafficking tends to mirror international trafficking flows, with victims moving from poorer, often rural, areas, to richer and more urban areas. When examining cross-national trafficking, victims tend to be from countries within the same region. Western and Southern Europe, North America, and the affluent countries of the Middle East are the only destinations with significant levels of detected victims trafficked from other regions (UNODC, 2020).

Through these reports, we can see that over the last 15 years, the number of detected victims has increased over time, becoming more equal among the sexes, with the share of adult women falling from 70% to less than 50% by 2018. Explaining why this split has become more equal over time, some scholars point to the shift from focusing solely on the sex trafficking of women to other forms of trafficking and victims, as well as increases in awareness and training. Children account for about one-third of the detected victims of trafficking and are disproportionately linked with the broader issue of child labor in low-income countries. Sexual exploitation remains the most common motive for trafficking at 50%, with labor trafficking representing 38% among detected cases, 6% subjected to forced criminal activity, and more than 1% to begging. Smaller numbers were trafficked for forced marriages, organ removals, and other purposes. Domestic servitude, fishing, agriculture, and mining are industries in which labor trafficking has been well documented. Such sectors also lend themselves to workers being isolated, making abuses difficult to detect and punish. Direct physical violence is rarely used to recruit victims, instead deception and targeting the victim's situation of need are used. After the recruitment phase, the use of violence is reported during the exploitation, alongside other means of control such as the confiscation of travel documents (UNODC, 2020).

Another source of data at a global level is the Counter-Trafficking Data Collaborative (CTDC). The CTDC is a dataset founded by the IOM with thousands of individual-level, anonymized entries about victims of human trafficking identified worldwide by counter-trafficking organizations. Because the data comes from identified cases of trafficking, it is important to keep in mind that the data may not be representative of the total victim population. As human trafficking is a crime intended to go undetected, identified cases are not a true random sample of the population. However, these cases do provide detailed data on the profiles, forms, and experiences of trafficking victims.

Data through 2021 shows that of the cases logged by the CTDC, 55% were categorized as sexual exploitation, 37% as labor exploitation, and the remaining 8% as other. Seventy-three percent of identified victims were female and 27% were male. The most frequently reported age category of the victims differs by type of exploitation, with ages 9–17 occurring most frequently for sexual exploitation and ages 30–38 occurring most frequently for labor exploitation. The victims' relationship to their recruiter is far more likely to be an intimate partner, family member, or friend for victims of sexual exploitation, while for labor exploitation the other category is most frequent. The means of control used on victims also share some differences by type of exploitation. The top five means of control reported by victims of sexual exploitation in order are: psychological abuse, threats, restriction of movement, physical abuse, and use of psychoactive substances. For victims of labor exploitation, the top five means of control reported are: taking earnings, excessive working hours, psychological abuse, threats, and restriction of movement (CTDC, 2021)

Qualitative research such as surveys and interviews conducted by researchers is another way in which we can gain detailed knowledge about the issue of trafficking. Reviews of the human trafficking literature have found that qualitative studies are more common, typically examining victims' exploitation and experiences with services (Russell, 2018). Qualitative studies tend to focus on smaller units of study over national or cross-national studies. This is advantageous because qualitative and quantitative studies of cities or even small regions can provide valid numbers about the extent of the problem and richer information about the experiences of trafficking victims (Weitzer, 2014). Such research can then be used to more effectively identify and target "hot spots" of trafficking for intervention efforts.

As one example, fieldwork and respondent-driven sampling of undocumented Spanish-speaking migrant workers in San Diego led to 826 participant interviews. Among this sample, 31% experienced treatment that meets the legal definition of human trafficking, while 55% experienced various abusive labor practices (Zhang et al., 2014). The most frequently reported violations were unfair labor practices (45%), deceptive practices (28%), physical restriction (22%), and physical threats (15%). Construction work, food processing, and janitorial/cleaning were the top three industries migrant workers reported experiencing these abusive practices in. This reflects the findings of other research, that forced labor frequently involves migrants in industries where the cost of labor is the primary means of increasing a business' competitiveness (Zhang, 2012). From their results, the authors then estimated the percentage of labor trafficking victims in the undocumented workforce of San Diego County to be between 26 and 35% (Zhang et al., 2014). While the authors note that such a local sample should not be generalized to the national level, studies like this are important in providing evidence that labor trafficking may be frequent among certain sub-populations or in particular industries.

There are also a variety of non-governmental organizations (NGOs) working in the field of human trafficking, providing services to victims, training to law enforcement, outreach to potential victims, and more. Such organizations can also act as a source of data on human trafficking. These victim service providers can be a primary source of data on how victims are referred for services (i.e., from the police, a hospital, or other sources), the services victims sought and received, and the demographic characteristics of the victims they serve.

In the United States, the National Human Trafficking Hotline, which receives federal funding, works to connect victims of human trafficking with the services and support they need. Tips about potential situations of trafficking are reported to the appropriate authorities in certain cases. Between 2007, when the hotline began, and 2019, the hotline received over 250,000 contacts about over 60,000 distinct situations of trafficking. Among the suspected human trafficking cases being reported to the hotline, one study found that the majority involved direct contact with a potential victim (40.9%), followed by observation of suspicious activity (25.4%), victim self-report (24.2%), and indirect contact with a potential victim (11.9%). Approximately 7% of cases involved a victim in immediate need, with the most common request being for emergency shelter (Tillyer et al., 2023).

Statistics from the hotline can give us a general idea of the picture of human trafficking in the United States, though, like official data, these only represent reported cases. Sex trafficking cases were more frequently reported to the hotline, making up 72% of all reports. Sex trafficking cases were more likely to involve female victims and minors, while labor trafficking cases were more likely to involve male victims and foreign nationals. However, labor trafficking cases involved greater numbers of victims, averaging 5.27 victims compared to 1.90 for sex trafficking cases (Tillyer et al., 2023).

The Media and Human Trafficking

Before reading this book, what do you think of when you hear the words human trafficking? What images come to mind? What does a victim of human trafficking look like and what do they experience? Perhaps you picture a woman held in sex slavery, imagine someone kidnapped and sold as in the film *Taken*, or worry that sex trafficking increasingly occurs online or in big cities during major events. While sex trafficking does occur, the reality of human trafficking is complex and multifaceted, though this reality is often obscured in the media. Both popular media and the news media have played a large role in shaping the societal understanding of this crime, even influencing human trafficking policy and legislation (Rodríguez-López, 2018). However, panics, conspiracies, and misinformation often abound in these media portrayals.

This book uses cultural criminology and moral panic theory to break down these panics, both historical and modern, to understand the impacts of media representations of human trafficking. By contextualizing crime within the cultural realm, we can understand the displays, messages, and meanings around human trafficking. This includes understanding the process by which people come to be defined as victims and criminals. The reactions to these social constructions of human trafficking are important to moral panics, where the reactions of the media, law enforcement, politicians, action groups, or the public are out of proportion to the reality of the issue. This book examines the impacts of human trafficking panics perpetuated through media, including understanding the origins of human trafficking in the nineteenth-century White slave panic, the reality of trafficking at sporting events, the role of social media in generating misinformation, and the ways that popular media perpetuates stereotypes.

Chapter 2 provides an overview of the theoretical framing that will be used throughout the book. This includes an introduction to social constructionism and cultural criminology. The chapter emphasizes the social construction of crime and the media's role in that construction. A brief history of moral panic theory is also discussed, including the components of moral panics, the role of moral entrepreneurs and moral crusaders, and theories about the origins of moral panics. Chapter 3 explores the origins of human trafficking panics with the White slave panic at the turn of the nineteenth century. The moral entrepreneurs, news coverage, and impact of the panic on legislation are highlighted before examining the panic's influence on the re-emergence of human trafficking at the end of the twentieth century. Lasting impacts of this panic are outlined, including trafficking's conflation with other concepts and criminal justice system impacts. Chapter 4 explores the role of pop culture in creating human trafficking panics, through television and films, campaigns, and celebrity involvement. Pop culture panics are explored for how they shape public beliefs and reinforce stereotypes about human trafficking. Chapter 5 turns to sporting event panics, with mega-sporting events such as the Olympics, World Cup, and Super Bowl believed to be hosts to human trafficking. The evidence behind such claims is explored, along with their impact on sex workers who are not trafficking victims. Finally, Chapter 6 looks at the ways that modern technology, and specifically social media, shapes human trafficking panics. This includes the use of hashtags and online social movements in generating misinformation as well as the role that internet plays in human trafficking and how legislation is trying to tackle the issue. Chapter 7 concludes the book with a review of how these panics have changed over time, and the implications these panics have moving forward.

Note

1 Portions of this chapter are adapted with permission from the following work: Hupp Williamson, S. (2024). *Criminology Explains Human Trafficking*. University of California Press.

2 Cultural Criminology and Moral Panic Theory

This chapter provides an overview of the theoretical framing that will be used throughout the book. The chapter begins by covering social constructionism, an important foundation to both cultural criminology and moral panic theory. The history and development of cultural criminology is then covered, with special attention to the role of the media. Moral panic theory is then explained, including its roots in labeling theory, critical concepts of the theory, and once more, the important role of the media. These perspectives are related and all contribute to understanding human trafficking, from the social construction of the issue to media portrayals to rule creation.

Social Constructionism

Social constructionism refers to a perspective that emphasizes the ways that social dynamics and social processes create and define various phenomena as social problems (Goode & Ben-Yehuda, 1994). Through analysis, this approach takes into consideration the ways that social facts are created, spread, confirmed, or denied. In regard to crime, this includes the relationships between social structures, laws, behaviors, and perceptions of those behaviors (Rafter, 1990). This approach frequently focuses on *why*, that is, why certain behaviors are problematized over others at certain times, why we engage in different methods of crime control, and why certain laws are passed.

The examination of social problems can proceed from two perspectives: an objectivist view or a constructionist view. An objective approach to a social problem would include consideration of the objective threat the issue poses. Conversely, a constructionist view recognizes that the issue may not exist entirely in objectivity. Instead, people act as a social force in defining what is a problem, and how much concern should be felt about a given problem (Goode & Ben-Yehuda, 1994). It is this second perspective from which social constructionism emerges and is frequently applied to the study of social problems.

Spector and Kitsuse (1973) state that groups or societies make assertions and claims about a condition, defining it as a social problem. Joel Best's

DOI: 10.4324/9781003439004-2

(2013) more recent work on social problems highlights the social constructionist perspective. He states that in the early stages of the social problems process, "constructing a social problem involves a process of claimsmaking: someone must bring the topic to the attention of others, by making a claim that there is a condition that should be recognized as troubling, that needs to be addressed" (Best, 2013, pp. 14–15). Media coverage is necessary to spread these claims to a wider audience and generate public reaction to pressure and influence policy. A typical claims-making process includes the use of extreme or dramatic examples, exaggerated or unverified statistics, and coverage of those accused of the harm and those affected by the harm (Best, 2013).

The history of social constructionism can be linked to other perspectives such as the sociology of knowledge and symbolic interactionism (Lindgren, 2005). Drawing on previous writings on the sociology of knowledge from scholars such as Mannheim and Merton, sociologists Berger and Luckmann wrote about the ways that reality is socially constructed by the actions of people. They asked questions about the social and cultural ways our lives and our knowledge about the world are intertwined. Customs, the function of institutions, habits, and meanings of behavior constitute knowledge stemming from our symbolic universes and are subject to different interpretations (Berger & Luckmann, 1967). The separate but related development of symbolic interactionism has roots in the work of Mead, who believed that different people can interpret situations differently based on the unique meanings they bring to their understanding of the situation. The meanings that people bring into these situations come from their interactions with others. As seen with social constructionism, interactionism emphasizes the meanings attached to crime and criminality, including the process by which people are defined as criminals or victims (Bohm & Vogel, 2015). An example of both perspectives can be found in the statement by sociologists Thomas and Thomas that "if men define situations as real, they are real in their consequences" (Thomas & Thomas, 1928, p. 572). This statement exemplifies how it is not the rule violation that is objectively criminal or deviant, but rather others' reactions to the rule-breaking that defines it as such.

Cultural criminology, labeling theory, and moral panics all share links to these perspectives. Cultural criminology draws on the social constructionist perspective to highlight understandings of crime and crime control, including the symbolic representations of crime in media (Ferrell, 1999). Similarly, labeling theory takes roots in social constructionism, posing questions about how criminal law is created and why (Rafter, 1990). Moral panic research simply extended the interactionist focus to examine the wider social context that created alarm and reaction to deviant and criminal behavior, while also stressing the role of media in the labeling process (Lindgren, 2005). Each of these theoretical perspectives is outlined in more detail in the following sections.

Cultural Criminology

The Roots of Cultural Criminology

Cultural criminology draws on a variety of other traditions, including symbolic interactionism, social constructionism, critical criminology, and perspectives on culture and subcultures (Ferrell, 1999; Ugwudike, 2015). Cultural criminology was considered one of the newest directions in critical criminology, and key proponents included the work of Katz, Ferrell, Presdee, and Hayward and Young (DeKeseredy & Dragiewicz, 2011; Triplett & Upton, 2015; Ugwudike, 2015). Originating in the 1990s, the development of cultural criminology was heavily influenced by the work of subcultural and labeling theorists in the preceding decades. Work from scholars such as Cohen, Cloward, and Ohlin in the 1950s and 1960s laid the groundwork for subcultural and labeling theory. In the 1970s and 1980s, British scholars in the Centre for Contemporary Cultural Studies at the University of Birmingham would provide further influence with critical attention to the role of media representation, power, and broader social structural dynamics as a whole (Ferrell, 2013; Ferrell et al., 2015; Ugwudike, 2015). It is from these foundational perspectives that cultural criminology was built, taking essential ideas such as:

> the understanding that deviance and criminality inevitably embody contested meanings and identities; the sense that all parties to crime and deviance—courts, cops, criminals, everyday citizens, media institutions—engage in cultural work as they negotiate these meanings and identities, work to assign symbolic status and attempt to find collective solutions; a sensitivity to the subcultural roots of crime and deviance, and to the meaningful process by which subcultural members confront their shared problems; and an awareness that, overarching all this, there is a web of larger societal values, carrying with them the tensions of failure and success, and the politics of inclusion and exclusion.
>
> (Ferrell et al., 2015, p. 41)

The above quote identifies several elements of cultural criminology that reflect the emphasis the perspective has placed on concepts like meaning, definition, identity, and symbolism, and how these concepts relate to the ways that crime and crime control are constructed collectively. In the early years of the theory's development, cultural criminology focused primarily on how this production of meaning related to subcultures, particularly subcultures that were stigmatized by the media. As the theory developed and took influence from British scholars, the critical aspects of the theory became incorporated, with an emphasis on how power relates to such construction (Hayward, 2016). Ultimately, cultural criminology can be conceptualized as a framework that is influenced by symbolic interactionism, social constructionism, critical perspectives on power and subculture, and the process of labeling. Together, these roots form a theoretical perspective capable of examining issues of meaning, power, and accounts of crime and crime control across various levels of the social structure, from individuals to institutions.

Defining Cultural Criminology Today

Today, cultural criminology lacks a single, precise definition. One scholar defines it as "an orientation designed especially for critical engagement with the politics of meaning surrounding crime and crime control, and for critical intervention into those politics" (Ferrell, 2013, p. 258). Another states that it involves the "placing of crime and its control in the context of culture; that is, viewing both crime and the agencies of control as cultural products" (Hayward & Young, 2004, p. 259). Both definitions emphasize the importance of culture within the study of criminology. This focus draws attention toward questions about who and what is labeled criminal, what we should be frightened of, and what we consider to be justice (Presdee, 2004).

One of the foundational concepts of cultural criminology is studying the influence that cultural dynamics and processes have on definitions and representations of crime and crime control (Ferrell et al., 2015). Culture is thus central to the theory. Culture can be defined in many ways, but cultural criminologists generally consider it to be "the stuff of collective meaning and collective identity… those threads of collective meaning and understanding that wind around the everyday…animating the situations and circumstances" (Ferrell et al., 2015, p. 3). While the study of culture—including the values, symbols, and emotions that are tied to crime and deviance—is a central component of cultural criminology, the structural is not ignored either. Drawing on the role of power, and particularly economic and political power, structural factors such as inequality are important in understanding how cultural definitions surrounding crime and crime control are shaped (Triplett & Upton, 2015; Ugwudike, 2015).

The Media and Cultural Criminology

Cultural criminology situates crime and punishment squarely within the cultural, examining their public and private displays, messages, and meanings (Muzzatti & Smith, 2018). The perspective critiques the process by which things and people come to be defined as victims and criminals. This includes the role of the media in constructing the reality of crime, with cultural criminology being known for making use of various methodologies to examine the content and discourse of various media forms (Muzzatti & Smith, 2018). Culture today is interwoven with technology, with information being constructed by the media (Triplett & Upton, 2015). This includes TV, music, movies, newspapers, and online media accessible via phones and laptops, all of which cultural criminology can be used to analyze (Ferrell, 1999).

A growing interest in understanding the media's role in constructing the reality of crime has also helped further develop cultural criminology (Muzzatti & Smith, 2018). This includes analysis of both news media and mass media. Newsmaking refers to the processes involved in the production of news, and newsmaking about crime refers to the ways that media interacts with information about crime and criminal justice (Barak, 1995). Gans (1980, p. 80) defined news as:

> information which is transmitted from sources to audiences, with journalists—who are both employees of bureaucratic commercial organizations and members of a profession—summarizing, refining, and altering what becomes available to them from sources in order to make the information suitable for their audiences.

Media formats, including news media and mass media, includes things as varied as "news background, documentary and docu-drama, realistic fiction such as TV soap operas, editorial comments, letters to newspapers, appeals for support, fund-raising efforts and media campaigns on behalf of groups, advertising in the media, and attention to talk shows" (Barak, 1995, p.17).

Cultural criminology is highly relevant to understanding the ways that media shapes perceptions about crime and crime control. This includes the ways that media distorts the reality of crime, emphasizing stereotypes and myths around crime. Portrayals of crime focus disproportionately on crimes that are interpersonal, violent, and sexual (Barak, 1995). Further, these portrayals are "severed from its underlying socioeconomic conditions; [and] disconnected from its own historical development" emphasizing individual factors over structural ones (Barak, 1988, p. 576).

Moral Panic Theory

The History of Moral Panic Theory

To understand moral panic theory, it is important to know that it stems from labeling theory, which likewise stems from symbolic interactionism (Ben-Yehuda, 2009). As discussed prior, symbolic interactionism was concerned with the role that meanings and identity play in social interaction and larger society. The perspective implies that the labeling of individuals by others impacts their self-identity and future behavior (Matsueda, 2014). Labeling theory then, focused on the role that social labeling plays in the development of crime and deviance, including the role of formal and informal labeling and stigma and discrimination (Bernburg, 2019). Influenced by the work of scholars such as Erikson, Tannenbaum, and Lemert, labeling theory was solidified as an independent perspective with the work of Howard Becker in 1963.

In particular, Becker made several important contributions to labeling theory including defining deviance from a labeling theory perspective and moving beyond social reactions to include the study of the creation and enforcement of rules (Matsueda, 2014). The rule creators, also referred to as moral entrepreneurs, are those that seek to bring awareness to a cause and influence legislation regarding that cause, while rule enforcers include those who enforce the rules once they are made, such as criminal justice officials (Becker, 1963).

Moral panic theory draws from the perspectives of both labeling theory and symbolic interactionism to understand representations of, and reactions to, social problems (Rohloff et al., 2013). The perspective was developed in the changing social and political times of the 1960s, and this meant understanding the processes involved in generating concern and even overreaction about the perceived problem and the resulting social and legal fallout (Rohloff & Wright, 2010). Incorporating concepts from the areas of crime and deviance, social problems, and collective behavior and social movements, moral panic theory examines the links between social structure, social process, and social change (Goode & Ben-Yehuda, 2009). To do so, the theory centers on the concept of moral panic.

While the term moral panic was first used by McLuhan in 1964, the concept was more fully fleshed out in the works of Young (1971) and Cohen (1972) and further developed from work that came out of the National Deviancy Conferences of the same time (Rohloff et al., 2013). In *The Drugtakers*, Young (1971) explored how moral entrepreneurs fed into concerns about drug culture to call for harsher laws and punishment. Similarly, Cohen's (1972) *Folk Devils and Moral Panics* examined the panic over two youth subcultures, the Mods and the Rockers, assumed to be a criminal threat to a seaside community. Demonized as dangerous delinquents, the panic resulted in increased policing and arrest of the youths. Both Young and Cohen's work highlighted how these panics reflected larger concerns over hippie and drug culture and youth violence (Tosh, 2019). Both books laid the groundwork for understanding the cultural and structural contexts from which moral panics emerge, including key agents, dynamic causes, and the resulting consequences.

But what is a moral panic exactly? The concept is a metaphor, as it does not actually refer to physical panic such as fight or flight. Instead, the concept focuses on the symbolic cultural elements that construct moral boundaries, defining what behavior is good versus bad. This construction occurs through actions such as "speeches, sermons, preaching, negotiations, arguments, debates, legislation, law enforcement priorities, agenda setting and the like, all focused on moral issues" (Ben-Yehuda, 2009, p. 2). These actions perpetuate the idea that some group, behavior, or condition, threatens the well-being of society. It is important to note however that the reactions of individuals are not in proportion with the real danger or threat posed to society (Goode & Ben-Yehuda, 1994). For example, in the late 1980s, it was alleged that a wave of horrific crimes and ritual abuse acts connected to satanism and the occult were being committed throughout the United States, claims that were repeated throughout the media despite a lack of evidence to support them (Jenkins & Maier-Katkin, 1992).

Today, Critcher (2008) argues that moral panic theory may be divided into two camps: a processual model influenced by Cohen (1972) and an attributional model influenced by Goode and Ben-Yehuda (1994). He argues that these two models differ slightly in their view of the media (active versus passive role), the agents critical to outcomes (government officials versus a variety of potential claimsmakers), and their conceptualization of language (wider ideological discourse versus claimsmaking rhetoric). While there may be various nuanced approaches to moral panic theory, the shared commonality among them is a critical analysis of the relationship between "the media, the state, moral entrepreneurs, agents of social control, the general public, and those labelled 'deviant'" (Rohloff et al., 2013, p. 2).

Critical Concepts of Moral Panics

While developed in scholarly work by researchers, the term moral panic has become commonplace outside of academia, used in both popular conversation and political rhetoric (Altheide, 2009; Greer, 2010). The concept has influenced the language used by politicians and journalists, to the extent that it has perhaps lost its original meaning:

> The claim that a social reaction is, in fact, merely a moral panic, has become a familiar move in any public conversation about social problems or societal risks. In an age of exaggeration, where the mass media regularly converge on a single anxiety-creating issue and exploit it for all it's worth, the utility of a negating, deflationary riposte is perfectly apparent. No wonder, then, that the term has become part of the standard repertoire of public debate.
>
> (Garland, 2008, p. 9)

It is important then, to outline the critical concepts of moral panics, as outlined by various sociologists and criminologists.

Reactions are a crucial element of moral panics. Cohen (1972) looked at how five segments of society reacted to the threatening behavior or condition, including the press, the public, agencies of formal social control, lawmakers and politicians, and action groups. While all groups act as key agents in a moral panic, the mass media was identified as one of the most important. In the early stages of a moral panic, the media is involved in exaggeration, distortion, symbolization, and prediction (Critcher, 2008). Action groups, or moral entrepreneurs, campaign to bring attention to the issue and influence those with power such as law enforcement and politicians. The actions of all of these groups together influence public opinion (Critcher, 2008).

Researchers have also studied the causes of moral panics. Frequently, changes in society, including the social, economic, or moral order, can act to trigger moral panics (Klocke & Muschert, 2010). Garland (2008, p.14) notes that "Threats to existing hierarchies; status competition; the impact of social change upon established ways of life; and the breakdown of previously existing structures of control—these are the deep sources of surface panics most often identified." In looking at where such panics emerge from during such transitions, Goode and Ben-Yehuda (1994) identify three possible theories: grassroots, elite-engineered, and interest groups. The grassroots model includes moral panics that originate with the general public. Elite-engineered panics include those that a small, but powerful, group deliberately generates concern over to direct public concern away from other, potentially more harmful issues. The special interest group model reflects Becker's work on rule creators and moral entrepreneurs. Here interest groups such as "professional associations, police departments, the media, religious groups, educational organizations, and so on, may have a stake in bringing to the fore an issue" (Goode & Ben-Yehuda, 1994, p. 165). In all three models, mass media plays an important role in sensationalizing and spreading coverage of the panic.

However, not everything that is sensationalized by the media qualifies as a moral panic. Some researchers have identified five specific criteria that define a moral panic, including concern, hostility, consensus, disproportionality, and volatility (Goode & Ben-Yehuda, 1994). The element of concern refers to how people will feel a heightened sense of anxiety around a situation. The hostility element is aimed at the group deemed responsible for the threatening behavior. Hostility often involves dichotomization, where the "responsible" group is depicted as evil while those concerned are on the side of good. This, in turn, leads to stereotyping of the "responsible party," such as how anyone appearing to be of Arab descent has been seen as a Muslim terrorist post-9/11, regardless of their nationality, faith, or connection with terrorism (Goode & Ben-Yehuda 2009).

Moral panics also have an element of consensus. To have a consensus, there must be some level of agreement that there is an issue. While not everyone in a population, or even the majority, has to agree about an issue, it must be widespread enough to garner attention. Disproportionality relies on the over-exaggeration of an issue. Here, facts and statistics about the reality of the problem are non-existent or greatly exaggerated, and there may be a mismatch in the attention that the problem is currently given when compared historically or to other, greater, issues (Goode & Ben-Yehuda, 1994). Finally, there is the element of volatility, which represents the sudden nature of moral panics. The concern over the issue may arise quickly and just as suddenly fade away, it may reappear over time, or become institutionalized. Whether or not the moral panic has long-term impacts, the "fever pitch" of these five elements are not sustained over a long period of time (Goode & Ben-Yehuda, 1994).

Why do some issues result in moral panics while others do not? Favorable conditions around a topic help in the creation and emergence of moral panics. These include the ability of the media to draw rival claims from various agencies and interest groups; a narrative that is accessible to the general public with identifiable heroes and villains; visual elements that can perpetuate stereotypes about the issue; and identifiable solutions, no matter how realistic they may be (Jenkins, 2009). Many topics may also fail to generate a moral panic. Jenkins (2009) notes that issues that involve new technology not well understood by law enforcement, legislators, or media; issues where control of the problem lies within one agency, limiting response competition; and issues that are overly complex may work to limit the ability of a full moral panic to emerge.

The Media and Moral Panics

Actors such as the media, the public, law enforcement, politicians, and action groups all share a part in taking a social issue and turning it into a moral panic, elevating and exaggerating the problem for varied reasons (Goode & Ben-Yehuda, 2009). However, the media plays a central role in both generating and communicating moral panics. The media may overreport, use sensationalized verbiage, or otherwise embellish the story to bring attention. The use of fear is a centerpiece of entertainment news, exacerbated by a 24-hour news cycle that emphasizes sensationalism (Altheide, 2009; Klocke & Muschert, 2010).

The growth of publicly accessible media from oppositional viewpoints has perhaps changed the consensus element of moral panics today. With a wider and more diverse selection of media available to the general public, moral panic messages can be more easily defused (David et al., 2011; McRobbie & Thornton, 1995). Others argue that the increase in media outlets encourages "a 'sound-bite' culture in which the instant appeal of the 'fear' frame encourages the exaggerated, distorting, negative and confrontational reporting of issues" (Critcher, 2011; David et al., 2011, p. 224). In fact, media responses around moral panics frequently ignore the core or substantial issues at the heart of the panic, instead focusing on exploiting "fringe" or "marginal" issues around the panic (Jenkins, 2009).

Still other scholars say this multi-mediated world means that moral issues may draw more polarized responses, taking on cultural, racial, religious, or even regional divisions (Garland, 2008). This does not mean that moral panics as traditionally defined no longer occur, but that many issues that now begin as moral panics may end up more in the realm of identity politics or culture wars (Cohen, 2011; Garland, 2008). Consider for example, political and cultural conflicts over gay marriage, illegal immigrants, or Muslim women wearing the hijab (Garland, 2008). Whether one takes the perspective that the media still plays a largely unified role in moral panic generation or believes that there are competing messages across various media platforms, it cannot be denied that mass media is an important vehicle for both claims and counter-claims regarding moral issues.

Conclusion

Ultimately each of these theoretical perspectives shares history and important perspectives on crime and crime control. Both cultural criminology and moral panic theory stem from a social constructionist perspective of crime, emphasizing the way that issues come to be defined as problems. Moral panic theory also draws from labeling theory, which shares many connections with cultural criminology as well. This includes roots in symbolic interactionism, a focus on interaction and the social construction of meaning across multiple levels of analysis, and the role that power plays in constructing and contesting such meaning (Triplett & Upton, 2015). Further, both cultural criminology and moral panic theory center on the role of the media in constructing new realities of crime, as well as generating new forms of crime control.

The applicability of these perspectives will be highlighted in the following chapters. From cultural criminology comes a methodological emphasis on media characterizations of crime, including news reports, images, and film and entertainment (Ferrell, 1999). This includes a critical analysis of how complex crimes such as human trafficking tend to be reduced to one-dimensional portrayals. Human trafficking as presented in mass media is disconnected from its relationship to a capitalist political economy, portrayed instead as an individualized issue. Further, these portrayals tend to perpetuate stereotypes about who is a victim and who is an offender.

Moral panic theory highlights the relationship between mass media and the criminal justice system, including the origins and stages of moral panics. The concept of moral panics has been hugely influential in the field of sociology and criminology, applied to studies on topics as varied as AIDS, child abuse, deviance, drugs, homosexuality, immigration, religious cults, school shootings, and youth violence (Critcher, 2008; Garland, 2008; Klocke & Muschert, 2010). As Goode and Ben-Yehuda (2009) point out, however, many moral panics are about sex. They note that:

> Sex is a special and unique sphere in which rules are abundant, and strict, within which the human drama plays out and the status of wrongdoing and even abnormality is applied … Elaborate stories are written and interpretations drawn by us about the meaning of sexual behavior. It is no surprise,

> then, that some of the classic moral panics … burst forth over the issues of homosexuality … pedophilia … pornography … sexual slavery.
>
> (Goode & Ben-Yehuda, 2009, pp. 18–19)

Thus, moral panic theory will not only be useful in highlighting qualities such as disproportion, exaggeration, alarm, and what crime control solutions are sought, but it will also be relevant to understanding the disproportionate emphasis of sex trafficking over labor trafficking. In the following chapters, the theoretical framework outlined here will be used to explore historical and modern perspectives on the relationship between moral panics, media, and human trafficking.

3 The White Slave Panic

The White Slave Panic

The White slave panic emerged during the nineteenth century in the United Kingdom, spreading to other European countries and the United States. Reports of British girls working in Belgian brothels in the 1880s triggered concern among religious, political, and feminist groups. But, it was not until the 1885 publication of a sensationalized series of investigative articles about juvenile prostitution in a popular London newspaper that the moral panic reached the general public and incited a campaign against White slavery (Doezema, 2010). Historians today dispute the extent of the "White slave trade," with research suggesting the actual number of cases was quite low (Doezema, 2010).

To understand the emergence of this panic, however, it is important to understand the historical context of this period. During the nineteenth century, debates about prostitution and sexual morality had been ongoing with heightened concerns about the spread of venereal diseases like syphilis and gonorrhea from prostitutes (Cree et al., 2014). There were two dominant competing views about how to deal with prostitution: those who wished to regulate prostitution through a state system of licensed brothels and those who wanted to abolish prostitution entirely (Doezema, 2000). At the same time, cities were considered the domains of men, and spaces that unaccompanied women should not be found in. As one author states,

> Etiquette kept women off of sidewalks; the law kept them out of urban spaces like restaurants without a male escort. There's a reason the word "streetwalker" is synonymous with "whore" … it was safe to assume that a woman who loitered too long on a public thoroughfare was a prostitute.
>
> (Blakemore, 2017, para. 5)

However, all of this began to change towards the end of the nineteenth century. The promise of better financial prospects and developments in transportation

DOI: 10.4324/9781003439004-3

technology facilitated large increases in migration between 1860 and the outbreak of World War I. Many of these migrants were women migrating from Europe and Russia to North and South America, South Africa, and other parts of Europe and Asia (Attwood, 2016; Doezema, 2000). It is against this background of changes to the family structure, women's growing independence, and threats to national identity during an influx of immigrants that the White slave panic must be analyzed. As one scholar states,

> the myths around "White slavery" were grounded in the perceived need to regulate female sexuality under the guise of protecting women. They were indicative of deeper fears and uncertainties concerning national identity, women's increasing desire for autonomy, foreigners, immigrants, and colonial peoples.
>
> (Doezema, 2000, p. 24)

Below, the moral entrepreneurs involved in the moral panic are explored along with the role of news coverage and influence on legislation.

News Coverage

As mentioned above, journalist William Stead published an investigative piece designed to reveal to the public a "serious social evil." The series, titled "The Maiden Tribute of Babylon," was published in the 1885 Pall Mall Gazette and made use of graphic detail and vivid imagery to reveal the occurrence of an organized trafficking in young English girls into brothels and prostitution the world over (Gorham, 1978). This included describing the "the rape of children who had been 'snared, trapped and outraged either when under the influence of drugs or after a prolonged struggle in a locked room'" (Gorham, 1978, p. 353). Stead also claimed that virgins were being sold for five pounds to wealthy aristocrats (Saunders & Soderlund, 2003).

Stead's piece was also published in the United States where it was widely read as well. Similar to the United Kingdom, it contributed to the emergence of a campaign against White slavery, along with additional books, newspaper articles, reports, plays, and films (Doezema, 2010). Additional publications in the early 1900s added fuel to the moral panic. In 1907, journalist George Kibbe Turner published an expose in McClure's magazine titled "The City of Chicago: A Study of the Great Immoralities." The piece detailed how organized crime rings were arriving in the United States and profiting from kidnapping and selling both native and foreign-born White women into sex slavery (Soderlund, 2002).

Books were also published on the topic. Published in 1912, *From Dance Hall to White Slavery: The World's Greatest Tragedy* was one such example. Chapter titles such as "The Tragedy of the Girl From the Country," "The Tragedy of Stefa, the Little Immigrant," and "The Tragedy of the Factor Girl" all warn young White women about the dangers of drinking and dancing leading them into a life of forced prostitution. According to one estimate, over one billion pages on the subject of vice and prostitution were written between 1900 and 1920, with White slavery being consistently referenced throughout (Haag, 1999).

In these types of publications, the portrait of a stereotypical trafficking victim begins to emerge. She is young, beautiful, and naïve—seeking a better life she is lured, deceived, or forced into prostitution. The narratives were exaggerated and sensationalized, combining "salaciousness with moral righteousness" (Doezema, 2010). Illustrations from a popular book of the time demonstrate these tropes. Ernest Bell published *Fighting the Traffic in Young Girls; or The War on the White Slave Trade* in 1910 which contained numerous lurid accounts about young White women falling prey to sex slavery. These images depicted trafficking as occurring when women traveled, answered job ads, or frequented places owned by foreigners. One illustration shows a young White woman meeting a man described as a White slave trader at the train station, with the caption "Danger" while another illustration shows a young White woman meeting a possible foreigner at an ice cream parlor, described as her "first step downward."

Even outside the United Kingdom and the United States, these narratives could be found. A Scandinavian novel that was translated into at least three languages depicted the story of how

> a young Danish woman, eager to get a job abroad, falls into the hands of unscrupulous villains who imprison her in a London brothel and eventually transport her to Turkey to be kept in the Sultan's harem. After this adventure, she sadly dies somewhere in Austria as her rescuers are not in time to save her life.
>
> (De Vries, 2005, p. 47)

Campaigns against White slavery focused on White women as victims of foreign men and emphasized the sexual dangers of venturing outside the safety of marriage and family to the "outer world" (De Vries, 2005).

Moral Entrepreneurs

Following the publication of Stead's "The Maiden Tribute of Modern Babylon," protests were held and local "vigilance" committees were formed across the United Kingdom (Gorham, 1978). In the United States, as many as 40 cities formed similar "vice commissions" to investigate the prevalence of prostitution and trafficking in women (Doezema, 2010; Lagler, 2000). One of these committees, the National Vigilance Association (NVA), was formed in 1885 in England with the purpose of protecting young girls from trafficking and prostitution. More specifically, their nationwide network of committees worked on things such as "investigating employment agencies advertising jobs for young women, instigating convictions for "immoral conduct" and brothel-keeping, publishing pamphlets and holding meetings on various moral questions, and, notoriously, prosecuting vendors of "questionable books and photographs," owners of theatres staging "improper productions," and exhibitors of "immodest works of art" for their "assault on public decency" (Attwood, 2015, p. 327). The male leaders of the NVA portrayed themselves as dedicated to rescuing innocent young girls ensnared by slave traders (Gorham, 1978). This rescue narrative is demonstrated in another illustration from Bell's 1910 book, which portrays a young White girl captive behind bars with her cries described as leading "worthy" men to start a crusade against vice and prostitution in the city. By 1899, the NVA had grown enough to launch an international organization, the International Bureau for the Suppression of the Traffic in Persons (Gorham, 1978).

Though there had originally been two competing views about how to deal with prostitution: those who wished to regulate prostitution through a state system of licensed brothels and those who wanted to abolish prostitution entirely, it was the abolitionist view that came to dominate during the White slave panic (Doezema, 2010). Feminist abolitionists joined with religious organizations and social purity reformers, all united by the goal of ending prostitution and White slavery. In the United States, women's groups, temperance organizations, religious groups, and medical associations similarly united to abolish prostitution (Doezema, 2010). Evangelical Christian groups were also heavily involved, both in the United Kingdom and other countries such as the Netherlands (Attwood, 2015; De Vries, 2005).

These moral entrepreneurs centered their concern around the narrative of innocent victims being forced into prostitution and sex slavery by "evil foreigners." The Whiteness of the victims often served a two-fold purpose: emphasizing innocence and purity metaphorically while also emphasizing state and national identity literally (Doezema, 2010). In the United States, the White slave panic embodied fears about eroding racial boundaries following the end of slavery and the changing face of immigration. In fact, the panic in the United States peaked between 1907 and 1914, corresponding to a period of greater immigration as well as the Great Migration when Southern African Americans moved North (Pliley, 2019).

While these victims were often depicted as White, this was not the only image of victims at the time. Immigrant women were featured in White slavery campaigns in the United States, though notably absent were Black women (Doezema, 2010). Still, there were distinctions drawn, between "true" victims forced unwillingly into prostitution and "guilty" victims who were complicit or chose sex work (Attwood, 2016). True victims were innocent, and this was established by stressing their youth, virginity, and naïveté (Doezema, 2000). Included in the "guilty" category were women who migrated to seek work in prostitution, in cities such as New York, Rio de Janeiro, and Buenos Aires

(Attwood, 2016). Organizations like the NVA typically viewed trafficked girls as "helpless and weak and ignorant," a misguided foreigner, while those viewed as complicit in their prostitution were "sexually experienced, morally bankrupt, lower working-class women who had migrated to the country to electively sell sex" (Attwood, 2015, p. 340).

Ideas about gender, class, and nationality were also influential in delineating deserving and undeserving victims (Attwood, 2016). The sexuality of middle and upper-class girls and women was viewed as more controllable due to their economic dependence, with working-class sexual mores seen as not very different. However, poor girls and women were seen as able to "flout the mores of society" and choose prostitution as an economic option (Gorham, 1978). Because of this, class often played into which victims were seen as true versus guilty.

In addition to innocent victims being constructed in opposition to the guilty prostitute, victims were also constructed in opposition to their trafficker. The traffickers were painted as foreigners, with immigrants, African Americans, and Jews being popular targets of blame (Doezema, 2000). This was largely due, in part, to the fact that this was a time of change, with the face of immigration increasing and changing. In the United States, immigration shifted from Northern European and Scandinavian countries to Southern and Central Europe, as well as Eastern European countries like Russia (Doezema, 2010). In cities like Chicago and New York City, the foreign-born population grew to 21% and 30% respectively, by 1910 (Blakemore, 2017). In the discourse of the White slave panic were fears over migration and nationality combined with anxieties around women's growing independence and the breakdown of family (Attwood, 2016; Doezema, 2000).

Antisemitism also grew during this period (Attwood, 2016). Journalist George Kibbie Turner claimed that Jews were responsible for prostitution in Chicago in a 1907 article, and behind White slavery rings in New York in a 1909 article (Doezema, 2010). In the United Kingdom, Jewish populations drew distinctions between those who were part of English society and recent Jewish immigrants from Eastern Europe. Anglo-Jewish individuals emphasized the foreignness of the new immigrants through their language, fashion, poverty, and importantly, their potential criminality. Essentially, in order to "secure their elevated status within the country, members of the Anglo-Jewish elite were compelled to act, publicly and boldly, to police the Jewish migrants it held responsible for trafficking" (Attwood, 2016, p. 119). This was done in large part through the establishment of the Jewish Association for the Protection of Girls and Women, which portrayed working-class women who left their duties at home to immigrate alone as "morally deficient" and likely to be trafficked (Attwood, 2016). In the United States, the White slave myth worked in conjunction with other racialized stereotypes to paint the picture of the trafficker. If Whiteness depicted innocence and purity, Blackness depicted "impurity, guilt, and vice" (Doezema, 2010, p. 86). This included the predominate myth that Black men were sexually violent and would rape White women. This belief was also associated with the rise in lynchings in the South in the 1890s (Doezema, 2010).

In their claims, these moral entrepreneurs repeated unverified numbers. In the 1885 "The Maiden Tribute of Modern Babylon," journalist William Stead claims that "London's lust annually uses up many thousands of women, who are literally killed and made away with—living sacrifices slain in the service of vice" (Doezema, 2010, p. 66). A booklet titled *The Dangers of A Large City, or The System of The Underworld: Exposing The White Slave Traffic* (*The Dangers of A Large City, or The System of The Underworld: Exposing The White Slave Traffic*, 1900) begins with a preface that states, "Thousands of young, innocent girls are trapped each year and sold like cattle to the highest bidder…Hundreds of fiends in the form of men are engaged in this form of work." In 1910, a Chicago district attorney stated "literally thousands of innocent girls from the country districts are every year entrapped into a life of hopeless slavery and degradation" (Doezema, 2010, p. 93). As mentioned previously, historians now dispute the extent of the "White slave trade," with research suggesting the actual number of cases was quite low (Doezema, 2010). Many foreign girls who did travel to the United Kingdom were not in danger of being trafficked. Yet many were subjected to surveillance, interrogation, and moral judgments (Attwood, 2015). This was due, in part, to the passing of legislation that, in the name of fighting White slavery, worked to control prostitution and women's migration.

Impact on Law

This societal concern about prostitution and its associated ills was not new to the White slave panic—instead the White slave panic evolved against this background. The Contagious Disease Acts enacted in England in 1864, 1866, and 1869 introduced a regulatory approach to prostitution that allowed police to detain women suspected of prostitution and force them to undergo a physical examination for venereal diseases (Doezema, 2000; Gorham, 1978). Feminist abolitionists and social purity reformers alike, however, believed that prostitutes should be viewed as victims in need of rescue rather than be regulated and controlled by the state (Doezema, 2000). With such groups seeking the elimination of prostitution, the associations and organizations that emerged from the White slave panic provided additional political support for this abolitionist approach. For example, after its formation, the NVA sought to ensure the passage and enforcement of the Criminal Law Amendment Act of 1885. This act raised the age of consent from 13 to 16, increased laws against prostitution, and criminalized male homosexuality (Attwood, 2015).

In 1899 in London, the First International Congress on White Slavery was held, attended by delegates from 12 countries. Another congress held in 1902 resulted in the adoption of the 1904 international treaty titled the

International Agreement for the Suppression of the White Slave Trade (Boris & Berg, 2014; Outshoorn, 2015). The 1904 treaty, signed by 13 nations, addressed only the recruitment of women for prostitution in another country through fraudulent or abusive means (Doezema, 2002). The treaty focused not on providing protections for women as victims, but on creating systems to investigate and, ultimately repatriate, foreign women who were suspected of prostitution (Lammasniemi, 2020). The 1910 International Convention for the Suppression of the White Slave Trade expanded on the 1904 treaty, now including recruitment for prostitution within a country's own borders (Doezema, 2010).

In the United States, the White-Slave Traffic Act, also known as the Mann Act, was passed in 1910. The Mann Act was passed at a time when the prostitution debate and the White slave trade were high-profile issues in the country. It was in response to the fear of "White slavery" specifically that Congress passed this act. The Mann Act prohibited unmarried women from crossing state lines for immoral purposes and its primary stated intent was to address prostitution, immorality, and human trafficking, particularly where trafficking was for the purpose of prostitution. In practice, however, the law's broad and ambiguous language about "immorality" resulted in it being used to criminalize even consensual sexual behavior between adults (Kakar, 2017; Lutnick, 2016). One study of 87% of the cases prosecuted under the Mann Act between 1927 and 1933 showed that 46% of cases involved women who identified as prostitutes and were arrested for aiding in the transportation of another woman across state lines for the purpose of prostitution, 23% involved women traveling across state lines with their boyfriend when one or both of them was married to someone else, 16% of cases involved women whose sporadic engagement in prostitution was to finance their travels, and 15% involved women who were working as prostitutes (Beckman, 1983).

The misplaced fears over White slavery that led to the passage of the Mann Act also led to the law being used to target and harass Black men traveling with White women (Chacón, 2006). This is demonstrated by the prosecution of heavyweight boxer Jack Johnson, a Black man who won the world championship from a White man. Doezema (2010, pp. 88–89) describes the case:

> In 1912 Johnson was brought before a grand jury on White slavery charges regarding a former girlfriend, a White prostitute named Belle … Belle, Johnson and a few other prostitutes had travelled together to and from Johnson's fights, living it up in cities including Chicago, New York and Minneapolis. During the trial, the state was unable to prove that Johnson had in any way profited from Belle's prostitution, or that he had "induced" her to cross state lines. Nonetheless, Johnson was convicted and sentenced to five years in prison.

The Ku Klux Klan even used the trial to try to prevent Johnson from continuing to box on the basis that he was a "White slaver" (Doezema, 2010). Through the Mann Act, the federal government was able to police women's movement and interracial relationships (Pliley, 2019).

Outside the United Kingdom and the United States, other countries passed legislation as well. Legislation passed in Greece in 1912 forbade women under 21 years of age to travel abroad without a special permit (Doezema, 2000). Italy used anti-trafficking measures to control women's migration and interracial sexual activity (Limoncelli, 2010). Overall, these cases show how early anti-trafficking laws were in practice not about women and girls being abducted and forced into the sex trade, but about the values and morals surrounding prostitution, national identity, and women's movement.

While the White slave panic had seemingly emerged out of nowhere at the end of the 1800s and quickly grown to great influence, it quietly faded out of public discourse in the early 1900s. Vice investigations that had been put together to estimate the prevalence of the traffic in women came up empty-handed. A 1910 investigation in New York City revealed the claims to be a hoax, while a 1913 report presented to the Massachusetts legislature "stressed that the 'large number of stories' which were furnished to the committee on women and girls being forced into prostitution were untrue" (Lagler, 2000, p. 355; Saunders & Soderlund, 2003). Newspaper editorials in New York City and Chicago began to distance themselves from such stories and denounce White slavery as a myth (Lagler, 2000; Soderlund, 2002). Other factors contributed to the die-down of the panic as well, including the outbreak of World War I which saw an associated decrease in immigration (Saunders & Soderlund, 2003).

There was additional legislation that was passed following World War I, though the language of White slavery was replaced with trafficking in women. Many international agreements were created under the predecessor to the United Nations, the League of Nations, and dealt with similar concerns about the movement of women. This included the International Convention for the Suppression of the Traffic in Women and Children (1921) and the International Convention for the Suppression of the Traffic in Women of Full Age (1933). The 1933 convention condemned all recruitment for prostitution or immoral purposes in another country and obligated states to punish it, even if the sex work was consensual (Doezema, 2010). This abolitionist stance on prostitution was repeated in 1949 when the United Nations passed the Convention for the Suppression of the Traffic in Persons and of the Exploitation of the Prostitution of Others. This convention called on countries to put an end to both trafficking and prostitution more generally, with a requirement that countries criminalize prostitution under national law (Lammasniemi, 2020). However, it was this abolitionist approach that led to many countries not signing onto it (Doezema, 2002; Outshoorn, 2005). Ultimately, there were many similarities between these early anti-trafficking efforts. The concerns that led to their passing were often rooted in racism and sexism, focusing on the prostitution of White women regardless of consent (Boris & Berg, 2014; Outshoorn, 2005, 2015). These early laws also did not formally define the term trafficking, focusing instead on the recruitment or coerced movement of women abroad for the purpose of prostitution.

The Modern Panic

It was not until the 1990s that concern about human trafficking would again reach a widespread audience (Saunders & Soderlund, 2003). Though it was now termed the "traffic in women" rather than "White slavery," many of the same themes can be found today. This includes motifs around youth, innocence, virginity, deception, and violence (Doezema, 2000). The threat of migrants, particularly those working as prostitutes, persists. However, rather than link prostitution with the dangerous vices found in cities, it is now connected with organized crime and terrorism (Doezema, 2010). By the early 2000s, a moral panic around sex slavery and sex trafficking was fully established (Goode & Ben-Yehuda, 2009). This section will explore the moral entrepreneurs, news coverage, and legislative impact of this modern panic, including its commonalities and differences with the previous White slave panic.

News Coverage

News coverage of the modern human trafficking panic has shifted over time, though some themes have persisted. When public interest in human trafficking as an issue first grew in the 1990s, it was discussed as a human rights issue, focusing primarily on the rights and needs of victims (Farrell & Fahy, 2009). This framing of human trafficking focused on women and children who were being commercially sexually exploited. This is when stereotypes about human trafficking involving physical force and the underground industry of brothels emerged. Analysis of news coverage of human trafficking across countries has consistently found a disproportionate focus on victims of sex trafficking, particularly women and children (Johnston et al., 2015; Marchionni, 2012; Pajnik, 2010; Sanford et al., 2016).

The 2000 passing of both the Trafficking Victims Protection Act (TVPA) in the United States and the United Nations Protocol to Prevent, Suppress and Punish Trafficking in Persons, Especially Women and Children (henceforth Palermo Protocol) enhanced public awareness of human trafficking as a criminal offense, prompting the media to take interest in this new crime. The narrative around human trafficking began to focus more on the progression of the act from beginning to end, including the recruitment, harboring, and transportation of individuals, rather than the conditions that make individuals vulnerable to human trafficking (Lee, 2011). This shift in media framing of human trafficking redirected focus from framing human trafficking as a human rights issue to framing it as a crime and criminal justice problem. Media focused not on the human rights abuses experienced by the victims, but on the illicit and dangerous nature of human trafficking operations. Human trafficking was framed as a problem of organized crime, leading to a focus on trafficking being connected to foreign victims and crossing borders (Farrell & Fahy, 2009). This is reflected in the fact that the Palermo Protocol itself is part of a larger protocol to the Convention against Transnational Organized Crime enforced by the United Nations Office on Drugs and Crime (Gallagher, 2010). These changes importantly tapped into public attitudes about anti-immigration and transnational crime (Chuang, 2006; Farrell & Fahy, 2009; Lee, 2011), and calls for stricter border control policies were often portrayed as the solution to human trafficking (Pajnik, 2010).

Across multiple countries, analysis of news coverage has found several commonalities. This includes stereotypical descriptions of victims as young, female, coerced, often foreign, and taken advantage of while seeking a better life (Gregoriou & Ras, 2018a). A typical narrative might involve a poor girl from a rural village or third-world country being "lured" to cities and Western countries where she is sex trafficked (Doezema, 2000). A Nepalese newspaper stated "Jewelleries (sic), money, fancy clothes and Hindi movies are luring girls to the cold city of neon lights away from the warm lap of the cool mountains" (*Kathmandu Post*, 27–10–1997) while a US-based Christian news organization said, "The Los Angeles activist wants to shed a different kind of light on the allure of this and other large American cities to young girls-from backcountry and backward countries alike" (*The Christian Science Monitor*, 12–03–98) (Doezema, 2000, pp. 34, 37). Traffickers are described as male, with their foreign nationality often highlighted, and ties to organized crime rings and criminal gangs are speculated on (Doezema, 2000; Gregoriou & Ras, 2018a). Further emphasizing the criminal justice lens, those who are quoted tend to be law enforcement personnel and government officials, with victims' voices rarely highlighted (Gregoriou & Ras, 2018a; Gulati, 2010; Sanford et al., 2016; Sobel, 2016).

An analysis of 80,000 news articles published in the United Kingdom between 2000 and 2016 found that trafficking was described in terms that emphasized prevalence such as epidemic, widespread, rampant, and influx. Further responses were often framed in reactionary and criminal justice-focused terms, as opposed to preventative and human rights-focused terms. This included describing trafficking as a war, something to tackle, combat, fight, confront, and purge (Gregoriou & Ras, 2018a). There is often a lack of attention given to the underlying causes and consequences of trafficking (Johnston et al., 2015; Muždeka, 2018). An analysis of US, UK, and Canadian newspapers found that when causes were identified, it was predominately criminal or law enforcement-related causes rather than political, socio-economic, or cultural causes (Gulati, 2010). Finally, sex trafficking stories dominate news coverage, with labor trafficking rarely focused on (Johnston et al., 2015; Marchionni, 2012; Sanford et al., 2016). This finding has held true even in cross-country analysis, including nations such as the US, India, and Thailand (Sobel, 2014).

Moral Entrepreneurs

As in the early 1900s, the moral entrepreneurs involved in modern human trafficking narratives include a broad variety of groups and organizations, with some reaching greater influence than others. This includes feminist groups, religious groups, and human rights organizations. As in the early 1900s, feminists remained split on the issue of prostitution, with some groups arguing that there is no such thing as voluntary prostitution, while other groups distinguished between voluntary and forced prostitution (Doezema, 2000). The former viewpoint is represented by the Coalition Against Trafficking in Women (CATW) while the latter is represented by the Global Alliance Against Traffic in Women (GAATW), two highly influential anti-trafficking groups.

The abolitionist feminist groups often worked alongside organizations of the religious right, including groups such as "Focus on the Family, National Association of Evangelicals, Catholic Bishops Conference, Traditional Values Coalition, Concerned Women for America, Salvation Army, International Justice Mission, Shared Hope International, Religious Freedom Coalition, and numerous others" (Weitzer, 2007, p. 449). Despite a lack of evidence to support their claims, abolitionist feminists believe prostitution and sex trafficking to be inextricably linked, deny the possibility of agency and consent within sex work, and believe legalization would worsen the situation (Weitzer, 2007). This narrative around sex work, and its conflation with sex trafficking, provides the avenue for such feminists to work with religious organizations also involved in anti-trafficking work. Weitzer (2007, p. 451) notes:

As the founder of Evangelicals for Social Action stated, the campaign against prostitution and sex trafficking 'certainly fits with an evangelical concern for sexual integrity. Sex is to be reserved for a marriage relationship where there is a lifelong covenant between a man and a woman.'

To generate widespread social concern and achieve political aims, moral entrepreneurs such as these continue to rely on presenting the most shocking and stereotyped stories about human trafficking, what one scholar refers to as "atrocity tales" (Weitzer, 2007). In Canada, a 2015 news series on sex trafficking describes victims as

> "beaten, branded with their pimp's name, and bought and sold across Ontario," … being burned with cigarettes, 'beaten black and blue, starved' until they service a certain number of men and having guns put against their heads or shoved inside their mouths. (*Toronto Star,* 2015b)
>
> (Roots, 2020, p. 105)

A photograph circulated in anti-trafficking briefings in Northern Ireland is described by the newspaper:

> A photograph showing how a woman forced into prostitution had tried to claw her way out of the room where she was being held in Northern Ireland was shown at a meeting of the Policing Board. The image was presented as a graphic illustration of the cost of human trafficking, as a senior officer said society needed to grasp the horror of the crime. [T]he officer said human trafficking was 'modern day slavery' and had to be tackled. (*Irish Independent*, 2011)
>
> (Ellison, 2017, pp. 200–201)

However, what is not noted in the news article, is that the Police Service of Northern Ireland had not actually identified any victims, and it was simply assumed that a victim was the source of the scratch marks (Ellison, 2017).

These sometimes exaggerated and sketchy claims are also connected with the repetition of unverifiable numbers about the extent of the problem (Weitzer, 2007). As discussed in Chapter 1, verifiable and accurate statistics on the number of victims are difficult to obtain. Global estimates of the annual number of trafficking victims that have been repeated in reports range from 600,000 to 4 million (Merry, 2016). One figure proposes an estimated 27 million people worldwide live in modern-day slavery (Bales, 2004). Despite the author of this estimate admitting it is merely a rough guess, the number has been repeated by evangelical Christian and secular feminist activists, non-governmental organizations, and even state agents (Bales, 2005; Bernstein, 2007). This large discrepancy between the claimed number of victims and the actual numbers of identified cases reflects the moral panic concept of disproportionality or the idea that the problem is blown out of proportion (Goode & Ben-Yehuda, 2009).

Another commonality between the two periods is that they both saw an increase in immigration that led to national anxieties. While immigration declined greatly following World War I, starting in 1989, there was an 11-year period of heightened migration into the United States (Saunders & Soderlund, 2003). Further, the feminization of international migration also grew, with female migrants now accounting for nearly half of all migrants (Doezema, 2000). With this, the image of the trafficking victim has changed due to the geographic shift in migration patterns. The White slave panic focused on European women forced into prostitution in the Americas and elsewhere, while today, the focus is on women trafficked to Western Europe and the United States from Latin America, Asia, and the former Soviet Union (Doezema, 2010; Saunders & Soderlund, 2003). There is also growing concern about rural to urban trafficking within countries (Doezema, 2000).

Despite these changes, much of the rhetoric around migration and trafficking is similar. For example, during the White slave panic, anxieties about the women's movement and increasing independence were reflected in posters that warned girls about going abroad or into the city (Doezema, 2010). Today, anti-trafficking campaigns reflect similar themes and warn about the "sexual dangers of life away from home and hearth" (Doezema, 2010, p. 126; Gregoriou & Ras, 2018b). Another thing that has continued is the distinction between what one scholar described as "innocent victims versus guilty whores" (Doezema, 2000). This scenario is described well by a journalist in Canada:

> The day they were arrested, last fall, they were the darlings of the media and a favourite porn fantasy, all wrapped up in one righteous story of salvation: 22 victims of "sex trafficking" liberated from their debasement in Toronto's suburbs by a carefully planned police raid. Everywhere… they were droolingly described as "sex slaves," conjuring up a vision of exotic but helpless beauties. A day or two later, police revealed that the 22 women, mostly Thai or Malaysian, had willingly come to Canada to ply their trade; wiretaps caught them boasting, long distance, about the amount of money they were earning. Public opinion did an instant about-face. Now the women were hardened delinquents, illegal immigrants, tawdry, dismissable, selling their bodies of their own free will. Phew! No need to fret about their fate. (*Toronto Star* 19–04–98)
>
> (Doezema, 2000, p. 36)

On the one hand, women from non-Western countries that fit stereotypical images of trafficking are seen as victims of their naïveté without agency in their decisions to migrate or even willingly engage in sex work (Doezema, 2000). On the other hand, migrants who do not fit the image of the ideal victim and are seen as willingly engaging in prostitution are stigmatized and criminalized (Gregoriou & Ras, 2018b). Research contradicts this viewpoint, with studies on migrant sex workers in Cambodia, Spain, and the Netherlands finding that few were tricked or coercively trafficked (Agustín, 2005; Busza et al., 2004; Vocks & Nijboer, 2000). While some expressed dissatisfaction with their working conditions, these migrants generally knew the nature of the work they were getting into and did so for economic reasons. This distinction between deserving and undeserving victims is further reinforced by laws that conflate all prostitution with sex work and frequently target sex workers under the guise of saving trafficking victims (Bernstein, 2007; Roots, 2020).

Impact on Law

As with the White slave panic, these moral entrepreneurs would go on to have a large influence over important legislation. Two examples of this include the US Trafficking Victims Protection Act (TVPA) and the UN Palermo Protocol.

Negotiations around the Palermo Protocol involved how human trafficking should be defined and what should and should not be included. Early drafts of the Protocol, submitted by the US and Argentina, presented a view of trafficking that reflected a very particular viewpoint. They referred to trafficking in women and children and explicitly linked prostitution to trafficking (Doezema, 2010). While the final Protocol uses gender-neutral language, the special status of women and children is still seen in the title: Protocol to Prevent, Suppress and Punish Trafficking in Persons, *Especially Women and Children.*

Two opposing approaches were found in the drafting of the Protocol. One centered on a law enforcement approach that emphasized protecting the state from crime, while the other centered on a human rights approach that centered on protecting the person from victimization (Doezema, 2010). The law enforcement approach ultimately won out. Country obligations under the Protocol are organized around three Ps: prosecution of the offender, protection of the victim, and prevention of the crime. However, the strongest terms are tied to prosecution as obligations, with substantially weaker terms tied to aspirations for protection and prevention. While it is *mandatory* that countries adopt legislation criminalization of human trafficking, it is only required that countries *endeavor* to take measures to prevent trafficking and *consider* implementing measures to protect and provide for victims (Todres, 2009). Wealthy countries had lobbied against obligatory language for protection aspects, "first, because of the perceived cost of providing aid, but also, more important, because of their fear of encouraging (illegal) migration to their countries" (Doezema, 2010).

In the United States, moral entrepreneurs such as abolitionist feminists and religious activists also influenced the drafting of the TVPA (Weitzer, 2007). Their influence is seen in the stereotypical narratives of trafficking repeated by politicians. For example, in a 2000 press release Representative Chris Smith (R) of New Jersey stated:

> Each year, 50 thousand innocent women and young children are forced, coerced, or fraudulently thrust into the international sex trade industry with no way out. This brutal, demeaning and disgusting abuse of women and children is predicated on their involuntary participation in sexual acts … The image of a young, innocent child being forcibly sold into the sex trade for the fiscal gain of one sick individual and the physical gain of another is tragic. The idea that we would allow it to go unpunished is even more so.
>
> (Chapkis, 2003, p. 925)

This statement reflects the themes that trafficking is solely about women and children forced violently into the sex trade, with their youth and innocence emphasized. Other narratives through the legislative record highlight stories of women and children, kidnapped or lured into sex trafficking. Senator Sam Brownback (R) of Kansas said on the 2000 Congressional Record:

> Force is often used in the cities wherein, for example, the victim is physically abducted and held against her will, sometimes in chains, and usually brutalized through repeated rape and beatings … Then the girl is transported across international borders, deposited in a brothel and forced into the trade until she is no longer useful having contracted AIDS.
>
> (Srikantiah, 2007, p. 755)

In response to these concerns, two anti-trafficking bills were drafted. One, supported by sex worker rights groups and members of Clinton's State Department, contained a broad definition of trafficking and distinguished between voluntary and involuntary prostitution. Under this bill, sex trafficking was simply one form of coerced labor. The other, supported by abolitionist feminists and religious activists, "focused primarily on sex trafficking with a few gestures toward other forms of forced labor" and claimed that the alternative drafting's focus on a variety of labor issues would "distract from combating sex slavery" (Soderlund, 2005, p. 73). The latter version was passed in 2000. Under the US TVPA, the term "severe forms of trafficking in persons" is defined as:

(A) sex trafficking in which a commercial sex act is induced by force, fraud, or coercion,

or in which the person induced to perform such act has not attained 18 years of age; or

(B) the recruitment, harboring, transportation, provision, or obtaining of a person for labor or services, through the use of force, fraud, or coercion for the purpose of subjection to involuntary servitude, peonage, debt bondage, or slavery.

Under the US law, trafficking into commercial sex is symbolically privileged over other forms of trafficking (Peters, 2013). Such a moral division has the outcome of minimizing and marginalizing the experiences and harms that labor trafficking victims experience (Barnhart, 2009). This separation has also had significant and real impacts on the way that criminal justice officials and service providers conceptualize what trafficking is and who trafficking victims are. A well-studied outcome of this separation under the law is how human trafficking is often reduced to sex trafficking, with training and resources prioritizing sex trafficking, and labor trafficking treated only as an afterthought (Peters, 2013). Sex trafficking cases are identified, investigated, and prosecuted at a higher rate compared to labor trafficking cases. This is not necessarily because there are significantly more sex trafficking cases. Instead, research shows a bias toward investigating sex trafficking cases (Farrell et al., 2020). This under-identification of labor trafficking victims compared to sex trafficking victims is likely due to a variety of factors, including definitional confusion between trafficking and smuggling, lack of awareness and prioritization of the issue among law enforcement, labor trafficking victims not coming into contact with the routine activities of police, and victims not coming forward due to being fearful of police and deportation (Barrick et al., 2014; Farrell et al., 2020). Law enforcement may not believe labor trafficking to be a problem in their jurisdiction or may not view labor trafficking victims sympathetically, believing that they wanted to come to the United States and therefore knew what they were getting into (Farrell & Pfeffer, 2014; Peters, 2013). Sex trafficking victims, on the other hand, are viewed through a moral lens, with their undocumented status being viewed as forced upon them (Peters, 2013). Further complicating the issue, this distinction between sex and labor trafficking under the law is also not always clear-cut in practice, as many victims of labor exploitation also experience sexual abuse as a form of coercion and control and exhibit similar forms of psychological trauma (Barnhart, 2009; Peters, 2013).

The TVPA also continues the distinction between "deserving" trafficking victims and "undeserving" illegal economic migrants. To qualify, victims must meet criteria such as proof of nonconsent and cooperation with law enforcement (Doherty & Harris, 2015). Deserving victims are assumed to have crossed borders under the control of their trafficker while undeserving victims cross borders due to situational push factors such as poverty or conflict (Srikantiah, 2007). In reality, the picture is often more complicated, as victims may have willingly migrated, even knowingly for sex work, though force, fraud, or coercion may have been introduced at a later stage. The lines between smuggling and trafficking are not always clear. Further, many victims may not wish to work with law enforcement due to fear or trauma. Individuals may have only one interview where authorities determine whether or not they are "authentic" victims. Hua and Nigorizawa (2010, p. 409) note that

> many tailor their stories to appeal to what federal authorities want to hear, such as the most abhorrent experiences they have endured, or sensationalized accounts (of being 'chained to a bed in a brothel') that will reaffirm authorities' pre-existing notions in order to prove that their victimization should take precedence over their status as undocumented immigrants.

The law can thus predispose law enforcement and social service providers to see "true" victims as an archetype of human trafficking, rather than a broad variety of possible experiences.

TVPA legislation also includes a clause that allows federal funds to be distributed to non-governmental organizations (NGOs) only if they make clear their opposition to prostitution (Ellison, 2017). For example, an organization that provides services that make sex work safer through things such as "street outreach, safe shelter, social services to assist with exiting prostitution, substance abuse services, health screenings, and access to condoms and dental dams to prevent sexually transmitted infections as well as various forms of contraception" are likely to be viewed as supporting prostitution and face funding restrictions (Nichols, 2016, p. 66). As a consequence of these stipulations, NGOs may tailor their aims in order to meet the requirements for funding.

This issue is not specific to the United States either. A study of federally-funded NGOs in Canada showed that the organizations used stereotypical images of trafficking victims and offenders in their materials and conflated sex work with trafficking. Conversely, organizations that dealt with sex workers' rights, migrant justice, and labor rights did not typically seek funding, likely because of restrictions that would alter their work (De Shalit, 2014). The pressure of foreign NGOs and the need for foreign aid resulted in Cambodia adopting a human trafficking law that reflected the US viewpoint, which widened the scope of human trafficking to include smuggling, illegal migration, prostitution, and pornography (Keo et al., 2014). True sex trafficking victims are rarely distinguished from consensual sex workers, with local authorities themselves involved in perpetrating violence, harassment, and illegal detainment against sex workers (Bradley & Szablewska, 2016). Another study of sex workers in Cambodia found that police crackdowns on brothels did not protect them but instead increased their exposure to violence and police harassment while decreasing their ability to access safe sex and healthcare services (Maher et al., 2015). Many countries' anti-trafficking framework cannot be separated from a Western influence that is embedded with stereotypes, misinformation about migrant workers, and gendered ideas about who is or is not a victim (Chow, 2020).

Frequently, a moral panic leads to a stage where law enforcement and politicians "crack down" and "get tough" on the activity related to the panic. Countries restrict women's migration, and police and deport sex workers, all in the name of anti-trafficking work (Doezema, 2000; Sharma, 2005). Northern Ireland saw crackdowns on brothels and commercial sex work, with immediate deportations for those involved (Ellison, 2017). Such crackdowns may deal with prostitutions but also migration and border security. For example, Cambodia placed limitations on travel rights in the name of curbing the trafficking of migrant labors to Malaysia (Kranrattanasuit, 2014). Specifically, the government passed a comprehensive ban on Cambodian women traveling to Malaysia for work in domestic service (TIP, 2012). Such restrictions can backfire, however, and instead increase risks for trafficking as migrant workers seek out risky routes or the services of smugglers (Kranrattanasuit, 2014).

Lasting Impacts

Having reviewed both the original White slave panic and the more modern re-emergent panic over human trafficking, many similarities can be drawn. Both periods reflected anxieties about migration and sexuality. Both panics reflected a very narrow view of who is trafficked and how. The youth and innocence of victims are emphasized, with those victims often being women forced into the sex trade unwillingly. Traffickers are portrayed as foreigners, with nefarious links to larger criminal rings. In response to these panics, laws were passed that often had additional consequences, including increased harassment of sex workers and restrictions on borders. There have been many lasting impacts of these panics, including blurring the definition of human trafficking by conflating it with other terms, perpetuating stereotypes about who is and is not a victim, and influencing the ways that the criminal justice system responds to human trafficking. Some of these aspects will be further explored in the following chapters. Here, the conceptual confusion around what human trafficking means is further explored.

Human trafficking is often conflated with related, but separate, issues. Frequently these include sex work, and prostitution especially, migrant smuggling, and slavery. The White slave panic made use of the phrase the "White slave trade" to garner widespread attention to the issue. One reason for this was that many of the moral entrepreneurs involved in the White slave panic had previously campaigned for the abolition of Black slavery (Cree et al., 2014). At the same time, the emphasis on the White slave was used to construct the issue as worse than its predecessor (Doezema, 2000).

Human trafficking has been referred to as "modern-day slavery" since the re-emergence of the anti-trafficking movement in the 1990s. President George W. Bush stated in 2002 that "trafficking is nothing less than a modern form of slavery, an unspeakable and unforgivable crime against the most vulnerable members of the global society" (U.S. DOJ, 2003, p. 1). Even modern legislation takes on this terminology, a recent example being the UK's Modern Slavery Act of 2015. Despite this push to frame trafficking as slavery, legal advocates have pointed out that, with the exception of only the most extreme cases, human trafficking does not meet the legal threshold for slavery under international law (Chuang, 2014). As Weitzer (2015, p. 227) states of the conflation between the two terms:

> Some analysts use the term slavery-like conditions to describe circumstances that are less comprehensive or onerous than outright slavery. These conditions include confiscation of legal documents, tight restrictions on one's freedom, poor working conditions, low pay, and debt that accelerates rather than diminishes over time. In this category, the worker does not suffer absolute slavery in terms of ownership, routine physical violence, total control, confinement, or dehumanization, but is subject instead to milder forms of control.

The UN 1927 Slavery Convention defines slavery as "the status or condition of a person over whom any or all of the powers attaching to the right of ownership are exercised." Slavery can be distinguished from human trafficking with respect to six elements: ownership, profits, availability, relationship, responsibility, and discrimination (Kakar, 2017). Under slavery, there was legal and documented ownership over the person that does not exist under the criminalized nature of human trafficking. The status of slaves was ascribed by the state, and assisting with their escape was criminalized (Davidson, 2017). Profits under human trafficking are much higher than under slavery—with human trafficking there is no responsibility over the maintenance of the person as they are seen as disposable due to a surplus of availability. Under slavery, the relationships tended to be long-term and more permanent, based on a discriminatory system that targeted minorities. Under human trafficking, relationships are short-lived, and all races and ethnicities are vulnerable. In this way, we can see that while human trafficking certainly bears some resemblances to slavery, it is important definitionally to recognize their differences as well.

Another common conflation involves equating sex work with sex trafficking. Given human trafficking's historical roots with moral concerns over the prostitution of women and sex trafficking, it is not surprising that this conflation continues today (Cockbain & Bowers, 2019). Stereotypes about human trafficking are replayed in media, with victims portrayed as innocent females lured into a life of sexual exploitation (Doezema, 2010). In regard to prostitution, it is the force, fraud, or coercion that separates human trafficking from criminalized sex work. Some sex workers may enter the industry willingly but become victims of trafficking later. While poverty, homelessness, and other precarious life circumstances may influence individuals' decisions to enter sex work, most individuals in the sex trade do not fit the statutory definition of human trafficking (SWAN & GHJP, 2020).

Modern human trafficking stereotypes also focus on the international aspects of the issue, leading to confusion between migrants who are trafficked and migrants who are smuggled. The UN Protocol Against the Smuggling of Migrants by Land, Sea, and Air defines smuggling as "the procurement, in order to obtain, directly or indirectly, a financial or other material benefit, of the illegal entry of a person into a State Party of which the person is not a national or a permanent resident." While human trafficking refers to a crime that is committed against another person, when we speak of smuggling, we are talking about a crime against a nation's laws regarding entry. Thus, one immediate difference between the two is that smuggling must involve the crossing of international borders while trafficking does not (Aronowitz, 2009).

Another difference is that human trafficking involves force, fraud, or coercion to carry out the crime—the victim does not participate willingly (Gallagher, 2010). With smuggling, the individual is generally a willing participant who is consenting to the movement. Once they are in the country, smuggled individuals are free to leave their smuggler, change jobs, and so forth (Stickle et al., 2020). While smuggling and trafficking are defined as separate crimes, in reality, they are often interrelated (Aronowitz, 2009; Scarpa, 2020; Skilbrei & Tveit, 2008). Deception and fraud may be used by smugglers to recruit individuals, blurring the lines of consent, and what may have begun as voluntary migration may turn into a situation of exploitation that the individual is no longer able to leave. Consider this story of a trafficking victim from the 2015 Trafficking in Persons Report:

> Over a period of several years, five Ukrainian brothers fraudulently promised 70 Ukrainians well-paying janitorial jobs at retail stores in the United States. They further lured the workers with promises to pay for their room and board and all their travel expenses. Once the workers arrived in the United States, however, the traffickers exacted reimbursement for $10,000-$50,000 in travel debts, making them work 10 to 12 hours per day, seven days a week to repay the debt, almost never providing compensation. The brothers abused the workers physically, psychologically, and sexually, and threatened to hurt the workers' families if they disobeyed. The brothers brought many of the workers into the United States illegally through Mexico. Over time, several new recruits were detained at the border and other victims bravely came forward, exposing the trafficking ring. Four of the brothers were convicted on charges of human trafficking; one remains a fugitive and is thought to be in Ukraine.
>
> (TIP, 2015, p. 48)

It is not easy to clearly separate the crimes of smuggling, labor trafficking, and sexual exploitation. With this case as an example, it becomes easier to conceptualize human trafficking as a continuum, "with the use of force and coercion at one end and voluntary movement for economic opportunities at the other end" (Derks et al., 2006, p. 32). It is in this middle ground that many migrants' experiences of exploitation may be placed.

Ultimately, this chapter highlights the origins of the panic around human trafficking. This is not to say that human trafficking is not a real phenomenon, or that action should not be taken against it. Rather, this chapter shows that the roots of the concern over White slavery, and subsequently human trafficking, build on stereotypes and extremes. The discourse that is echoed by activists, politicians, and journalists has also frequently resulted in the stigmatization, restriction, and criminalization of the groups they aim to protect. These issues will be explored deeper in the following chapters.

4 The Pop Culture Panic

Popular culture includes the most accessible and commonly shared aspects of culture. That is, it refers to the practices, beliefs, and objects that are most widely consumed by the public. It includes books, movies, television, music, fashion, and more. In the context of this chapter, the focus will remain on mass media formats of pop culture. Media formats, including news media and mass media, include things as varied as "news background, documentary and docu-drama, realistic fiction such as TV soap operas, editorial comments, letters to newspapers, appeals for support, fund-raising efforts and media campaigns on behalf of groups, advertising in the media, and attention to talk shows" (Barak, 1995, p.17). This chapter will cover the portrayals of human trafficking in television and film, the role of celebrities in anti-trafficking campaigns, and the consequences of how pop culture shapes beliefs about human trafficking.

It is first important to note that this is not a new phenomenon. In addition to news coverage of the topic, pop culture portrayals of human trafficking during the White slave panic could be found in books, films, and plays of the period (Doezema, 2010). Books often blurred the lines between sensationalized fictional stories and supposedly true, journalistic accounts. This includes books such as *The House of Bondage*, a bestseller by Reginald Wright Kauffman published in 1911, and *From Dance Hall to White Slavery: The World's Greatest Tragedy* published in 1912 (Blakemore, 2017; Goode & Ben-Yehuda, 2009). In addition to novels about captivity and forced prostitution, White slave films were also popular (Saunders & Soderlund, 2003). Two popular films released in 1913 include *Traffic in Souls* and *The Inside of the White Slave Traffic* (Hackett, 2022). Diffee (2005, p. 414) notes that the success of *Traffic in Souls* "rode on the tide of sensation that had already entered the entertainment industry through a rash of Broadway shows such as *The Lure, The Traffic, The Fight, The Battle,* and *The House of Bondage*. The film tells the story of a young candy shop worker who becomes trapped in a prostitution ring, only to be saved by her sister and a police officer. Over 30,000 people saw the film during its first week showing in New York City, and it would go on to gross over $450,000 and influence the production of additional

DOI: 10.4324/9781003439004-4

films (Diffee, 2005). However, as the White slave panic faded from discourse and news coverage, so did it begin to disappear from popular culture.

Pop Culture Portrayals

Victims, Villains, and Rescuers

As news coverage of human trafficking resumed at the beginning of the twenty-first century, so did media portrayals. In the early 2000s, human trafficking quickly became a hot topic and a "sexy plot line for films and television shows" (Austin & Farrell, 2017, p. 1). Myths are reinforced by this media, including that human trafficking is only about sexual exploitation, victims are White women and girls while traffickers are men, and the issue of trafficking is rooted in other cultures, while the rescuers are American (Todres, 2016). An analysis of 24 television episodes, 24 movies, and 43 documentaries about human trafficking demonstrates many of these stereotypes, with 68% focusing on sex trafficking (Austin, 2016). Television episodes and movies were more likely to portray organized crime as the cause of human trafficking with the solution being law enforcement, and more likely to portray predominately White victims who experienced physical violence and kidnapping (Austin, 2016).

Media representations of human trafficking have consistently stereotyped what both victims and villains look like, contributing to the idea of both the "ideal victim" and the "ideal offender." The concept of the ideal victim was first described by Christie (1986),and involved a weak and blameless victim taken advantage of by an evil stranger (Hoyle et al., 2011). These elements are reflected in the construction of the ideal trafficking victim historically and in popular culture today. The ideal trafficking victim is a victim of sex trafficking, female, and young. She also lacks agency, with victims not choosing to participate in sex work, and therefore being helpless and blameless (Rodríguez-López, 2018). A typical trafficking narrative may sensationalize the violence experienced by a girl lured to the West by the promise of a job or marriage, her innocence emphasized through her youth and virginity (Doezema, 2000). Such portrayals evoke more outrage and sympathy than the story of an illegal migrant or prostitute who finds themselves in a trafficking situation (Doezema, 2000). The story of "Christina" at anti-trafficking rallies in the early 2000s reflects many of these characteristics:

> The keynote speaker at an event described Christina as a young woman lured by the promise of a babysitting job, who was ultimately forced to work in a brothel … Bernstein [the scholar who documented the story in her field notes] notes that she heard this story retold a number of times with only minor differences … She also found that the Department of Justice had no record of any prosecuted cases with a victim matching Christina's

> description. As with the iconic victims of the white slavery epidemic, the facts of Christina's story were less important than her role in a narrative to drive a particular brand of reform.
>
> (Balgamwalla, 2016, pp. 16–17)

These narrow constructions often do not reflect the lived experiences of trafficking victims. The ideal victim lacks agency and is portrayed as totally blameless. In reality, many trafficking victims may play an active role in the trafficking and may be unwilling to testify against their trafficker (Boggiani, 2015). The ideal victim is forced across the border under the control of their trafficker and is not driven to cross borders because of factors like poverty (Srikantiah, 2007). Many victims may have crossed borders as voluntary migrants only to be later exploited, thus not fitting into the narrow conception of a naïve and passive victim taken against their will.

Nor does the concept of the "ideal offender" reflect the reality of traffickers. Traffickers are stereotyped as male foreigners with no known relationship to their victims who use physical force to control them (Raby & Chazal, 2022). In reality, research shows that traffickers are often known to the victim, as employers, friends, relatives, or intimate partners (Viuhko, 2018). Rather than evil figures enmeshed in organized crime rings, offenders often come from a similar background as victims. One study of traffickers in Vietnam shows that much like their victims, traffickers were poor, ethnic minorities with little educational or income opportunities (Le & Wyndham, 2022). Further, portrayals of traffickers are frequently associated with organized crime and mafia-like criminal gangs that are involved in sex trafficking (Doezema, 2000; Rodríguez-López, 2018; Urban & Arends, 2018). This is despite the fact that there is a lack of clear evidence about the relationship between organized crime and human trafficking (Lee, 2011). Research does not show a clear-cut consensus about the extent of organized criminal groups' involvement in human trafficking (Tripp & McMahon-Howard, 2016). Much of this research lacks sound methodology and empirical evidence or is significantly dated (Tripp & McMahon-Howard, 2016; Vermeulen et al., 2010).

Finally, in addition to "the innocent victim" and "the evil offender," there is the stereotypical "good rescuer" (Balgamwalla, 2016). Rescuers are frequently portrayed as American in contrast to the foreign trafficker. They also frequently work in law enforcement. Raids are a common method of rescue, though such arrests have been criticized for not resulting in identifying and assisting trafficking victims (Balgamwalla, 2016). While raid and rescue methods are discussed further in Chapter 5, it is important to note that raids have resulted in many harms, including

> the criminal prosecution of those exploited for sex, the detention and forced migration of those exploited for labor, the sensationalization and perpetuation of myths about human trafficking in the media, the commodification

> of trafficking as a revenue generator for private organizations, the emphasis on sex trafficking over labor and other types of exploitation, and many more.
>
> (Gagnon, 2020, p. 96)

Pop culture mediums such as film and television frequently make use of these stereotypes and tropes which act as "shorthand" for viewers. Audiences view these simplified versions of victims, villains, and rescuers and come to associate them with a true picture of human trafficking (Hackett, 2022). In the next several sections, the narratives of trafficking presented in films, documentaries, and literature are reviewed.

Fictional Films

Many pop culture portrayals of human trafficking follow the plot of a melodrama, which includes sensationalism and suspense, exaggerated emotion, contrasting characters such as heroes and villains, and an individualistic nature that often emphasizes an action hero who solves the problem over structural and societal solutions (Doezema, 2000; Hackett, 2022). Additionally, human trafficking films frequently focus on extreme forms of sex trafficking, such as the story of "an innocent and naïve young woman or girl is tricked or abducted by a villainous trafficker, who imprisons her and controls her with brutal violence until a heroic rescuer… overcomes tremendous adversity in order to save the female" (Baker, 2014, p. 209). In addition to gender stereotypes about the victims, villains, and rescuers, racial stereotypes are often present as well, with victims and rescuers frequently being White and Western, and the villains being men of color from non-Western countries (Baker, 2014). The problem of sex trafficking is solved when the victim is rescued, with the broader causes of trafficking, such as globalization, inequality, and oppression, are overlooked. The Hollywood films of *Taken* (2009) and *Trade* (2007) exemplify these tropes well.

Both *Taken* and *Trade* involve a storyline where the heroes race to save the virginity of the victims (Austin, 2016; Szörényi & Eate, 2014). In *Taken*, an American teenager travels to Paris with a friend, where she is discussing losing her virginity prior to being taken (Baker, 2014). She is abducted by Albanian traffickers and sold to an Arab sheikh, before being rescued by her father, a former CIA operative (Szörényi & Eate, 2014). *Taken* was highly successful at the box office, grossing over $225 million worldwide and eventually becoming a trilogy with a second movie released in 2012 and a third in 2014 (Todres, 2016).

In *Trade*, a 13-year-old Mexican girl is kidnapped by an international trafficking ring to be sold in an online auction for sexual exploitation. Her virginity is emphasized in a scene in which her brother explains to law enforcement that "'She's pure. She's never… '" (Baker, 2014, p. 212). The victim "is mothered by a fellow captive, Veronica, a gorgeous blonde Eastern European single mother who fell into the hands of the traffickers while trying to find work in the USA through a bogus employment agency" (Szörényi & Eate, 2014, p. 618). Interestingly, it is Veronica's face that appears on several promotional posters and DVD covers. With the help of a White, Texan cop, her brother works to rescue her from the Mexican and Russian villains (Baker, 2014).

Such films often deny victims any agency in their plots. Instead, kidnapped and abducted victims are portrayed as "drugged and half-conscious, constantly under threat of violence and violation" (Baker, 2014, p. 212). These films border on voyeurism, with scenes of rape and physical beatings. For example, the 2002 Swedish film *Lilja 4-Ever* tells the story of a 16-year-old girl trafficked by Eastern Europeans into Sweden, where several scenes depict her experiencing violence and rape before committing suicide (Arthurs, 2012; Small, 2012). Despite being fictional and based on little research, the movie became popular in education campaigns, with screenings held by several NGOs in the former Soviet Union and across southeastern Europe (Small, 2012). The Lifetime movie *Human Trafficking* has similar gratuitous sexual details:

> Helena, one of the Eastern European victims, falls captive in a Viennese mansion after her suitor lures her to Austria, steals her passport, and then sells her to traffickers. The kidnappers force her into an opulent hall lined with ragged young women on makeshift cots. One of the ruthless guards shoves Helena on the ground, pushes up her skirt, and rips off her underwear. He holds her down and rapes her in front of a dozen other people. Helena cries, sprawled on a dirty pillow, her bare ass in the air, with the man straddling her, and then the scene cuts to Manila.
>
> (Small, 2012, p. 424)

Produced in cooperation with the Department of Homeland Security, it is perhaps not surprising that an ICE agent who conducts brothel raids is the rescuer (de Villiers, 2016). Scenes that emphasize physical and sexual violence in a voyeuristic manner sensationalize the immediate suffering of the victim. This often involves oversimplifying of the issue rather than portraying the complex reasons that lead to trafficking victimization and the agency involved in the choices of many victims (Arthurs, 2012). Further, these films have an impact outside of pop culture, influencing beliefs about what human trafficking looks like and shaping political discourse (Small, 2012; Todres, 2016). One Eswatini ambassador to the United States cited *Human Trafficking* as an example of the "'brutal realities behind the international trafficking of women and children for sex'" (Small, 2012, p. 436).

More recently, the 2023 film *Sound of Freedom* has received criticism from anti-trafficking activists and organizations. Another sensationalized story about abductions and child trafficking, the movie follows a former government agent seeking to rescue children from a Colombian sex trafficking ring (Dickson, 2023). Anti-trafficking advocates worry that the film perpetuates misinformation about what trafficking actually looks like and what services victims actually need (Dickson, 2023; Merlan, 2023).

Documentaries

In some respects, documentaries, perhaps due to their non-fictional portrayals of human trafficking, rely somewhat less on stereotypes. One study found that minority victims are more likely to be present in documentaries than in fictional television and film, with documentaries also emphasizing the complex causes of trafficking, such as poverty, demand, and vulnerability (Austin, 2016). Still, documentaries may also reinforce many human trafficking stereotypes and follow a melodramatic, or as one researcher calls it, a melomentary narrative (Stiles, 2018). This includes a primary focus on sex trafficking, stereotypes about victims and offenders, and rescue plotlines.

For example, *Nefarious: Merchant of Souls* (2011) uses reenactments to depict mafia members punishing and controlling trafficked women, with the traffickers ultimately arrested and the victims rescued (Stiles, 2018). Similarly, *The Abolitionists* (2016) documents an American anti-trafficking foundation that conducts stings and raids to arrest sex traffickers and rescue victims in countries like Haiti and Colombia (Stiles, 2018).

Further, while non-White victims may be represented more, there is often still a hierarchy of victims, differentiating between those deserving of sympathy and assistance and those undeserving. In the documentary *Tricked* (2013), "all the White female survivors were labeled at the bottom of the screen as 'former sex slave' while minority women were labeled 'prostituted woman'" (Austin, 2016, p. 51). Documentaries like *Tricked* also blur the lines between trafficking and prostitution, often equating them together (Stiles, 2018). While documentaries can paint a more diverse picture of trafficking, they can also still fall into the same narrative patterns and tropes as fictional films. It is also important to remember that documentaries are less widespread and accessed in popular culture compared to film and television (Austin, 2016).

Literature

Books also reflect many of these same stereotypes, with crime fiction focusing on transnational sex trafficking (Beyer, 2018). This includes Stuart Neville's *Stolen Souls* (2011), a part of a series that follows a detective and tells the story of a young Ukrainian woman promised work in Ireland, only to be sold to a brothel run by an Eastern European organized crime group. Marnie Riches' *The Girl Who Walked in the Shadows* (2015) includes one plotline about the kidnapping of children and one about the transnational sex trafficking of children from Eastern Europe. Child kidnapping and trafficking are also found in Ruth Dugdall's *Nowhere Girl* (2015), and the rescue of a child trafficking victim is the plot of Agnete Friis' *The Boy in the Suitcase* (2011).

Even comics have been examined for their portrayal of human trafficking. Researchers have found human trafficking plots in the comic series Wonder Woman, Punisher, Wolverine, Ghost Rider, Batman, and Unknown Soldier (Benton & Peterka-Benton, 2012). Among the seven comic books they examined, five focused on sexual exploitation, four involved forced abduction, and all emphasize the use of violence to solve the issue.

Campaigns

The narratives, stereotypes, and images of human trafficking found in the media may also be used by organizations. The discourse perpetuated by anti-trafficking organizations then has the potential to influence policy (De Shalit, 2014). An examination of the language and images used by 18 Canadian anti-trafficking organizations showed several stereotypes, including equating sex work with trafficking, depictions of bondage through images of chains, ropes, and bars, and a focus on foreign women and children in need of rescue (De Shalit, 2014). Campaigns can be a useful tool for anti-trafficking organizations, seeking to educate the general public and even influence political agendas. This can include posters, brochures, billboards, flyers, stickers, and radio and television ads. However, many of these campaigns can also make use of a narrow view of human trafficking, with simplified depictions of victims and villains.

Materials analyzed from governmental, non-governmental, and corporate anti-trafficking campaigns in Europe, North America, and Australia recreated many of the tropes that make up the ideal victim and ideal offender (O'Brien, 2013, 2016). This includes depicting a young female victim, abducted or deceived into forced prostitution. For example, "The Truth Isn't Sexy" campaign endorsed by the United Kingdom Human Trafficking Centre and Crime Stoppers told the story of a girl "abducted from Albania and forced into prostitution" (O'Brien, 2016, p. 209). These campaigns disproportionately focused on female victims over male victims and sexual exploitation over labor (O'Brien, 2013, 2016; O'Brien & McLeod, 2011). Villains are individualized, including "organized crime gangs and the socially undesirable johns" (O'Brien, 2016, p. 208).

Campaign images may also depict passive, helpless, and violated female bodies that are often sexualized (Andrijasevic 2007; O'Brien 2013; Szablewska & Kubacki 2018). For example, in one image from a 2001 Ukrainian IOM campaign, a naked female figure is caught in a spider web, the nakedness is meant to depict the helplessness and vulnerability of trafficked women according to an IOM official (Andrijasevic, 2007). Such images are able to capture more attention and generate more support (O'Brien, 2013). For example, a study of 44 human trafficking awareness videos from 33 US agencies showed that they relied more on emotional appeals, with few references to statistics, evidence, or other factual resources (Preble et al., 2016).

As with the White slave panic of the early twentieth century, many modern campaigns also discourage migration and especially women's migration. Specifically women's migration is often portrayed as dangerous, leading to forced prostitution, and so the safe solution is to simply remain at home (Andrijasevic, 2007; O'Brien, 2013; Szablewska & Kubacki, 2018). For example, an IOM campaign run in the Czech Republic from 1998 to 1999 used images and stories of women who had a desire to work abroad, in industries such as entertainment, waitressing, fashion/modeling, and care work. Instead, the narratives tell that these women were deceived and forced into prostitution. The headlines for the campaigns included phrases such as "'Are you sure you know what's waiting for you?' and 'Do you think it could never happen to you?'" (Andrijasevic, 2007, p. 27). Rather than recognize the economic drivers of migration and agency exercised by many seeking opportunity elsewhere, such campaigns instead portray migrants as naïve to the dangers of migration, equating it with trafficking (Szablewska & Kubacki, 2018). This reinforces the idea that stricter border controls will solve the problem, when in reality they simply leave migrants more vulnerable to exploitation.

Many of these campaigns also focus on individualistic solutions that are charity based. Concerned citizens may be instructed to buy items to fundraise, donate money, or purchase goods made by trafficking survivors (Musto, 2009). For example, an NGO in Vietnam "rescued" trafficking victims, many of whom were actually consenting sex workers. Many of the women compared the experience to jail: "Their daily lives were structured by strict rules and routines. They were confined inside facilities with private guards who locked the doors and slept right outside at night to catch those who tried to escape" (Hoang, 2016, p. 28). As part of their rehabilitation, the women worked 10 hours per day and were paid $10 for each piece of clothing they sewed, which was then sold abroad for $100 as fair trade clothing (Hoang, 2016). While fundraising is often necessary, this focus on individual purchases to make a difference means that broader discussions around reforming immigration or enhancing labor protections are not included. When the problem of human trafficking is framed as bad individuals or even a problem of organized crime, root causes like globalization, poverty, demand for cheap labor, conflict, and discrimination are overlooked.

Celebrities and Anti-Trafficking Activism

In the past several decades, many celebrities have also become involved in anti-trafficking campaigns and other forms of activism. Celebrities may endorse campaigns and organizations, serve as ambassadors for governmental and non-governmental organizations, present themselves as experts, and even start their own foundations. A study of celebrities who engaged in anti-trafficking activism between 2000 and 2016 identified 282 celebrities, though most were only involved in one low-effort event such as attending a fundraiser (Majic, 2023). The majority of the identified celebrities were actors, White, with women involved more than men (Majic, 2023). Many celebrity campaigns also focus only on the sex trafficking of women and children and feed into the rescue narrative (Chuang, 2010; Haynes, 2014; Kempadoo, 2015).

The involvement of celebrities can bring more media coverage and public attention, as well as generate more funding. However, a review of celebrity involvement in anti-trafficking campaigns found that:

> The data strongly suggest that although a great deal of money and attention are directed to their "awareness raising" efforts, celebrity engagement is not significantly advancing the work of eradicating human trafficking. Instead, most celebrity activists reduce the complexity of both the problem and its potential solutions to sound bites, leading the public to believe that "doing something"—anything at all—is better than doing nothing, when the opposite may well be true.
>
> (Haynes, 2014, p. 40)

Celebrities may lack the knowledge and expertise to speak to the complexities of human trafficking, resulting in the sharing of misguided and questionable information (Cojocaru, 2015; Haynes, 2014). For example, as part of his work with his foundation, actor Ashton Kutcher cited bad statistics from a flawed report, stating that 100,000 to 300,000 children in the US became sex slaves every year (Conklin et al., 2011). Those numbers were from a 2001 report that merely estimated child sex trafficking based on categories of risk, where an "at-risk" individual could be counted more than once (Kessler, 2021). Celebrities may be more focused on presenting a quick and concise emotional appeal to the public, rather than on addressing the complex, structural issues and lack of verifiable data associated with human trafficking.

Due to their status, celebrities may also have the ear of politicians who may consult with them for policy guidance (Haynes, 2014). For example, in his testimony before Congress, singer Ricky Martin stated that

> "each year 2 million people are victims of human trafficking. Of those, 1 million children are forced into the sex trade each year" (Martin, 2006, 11). These figures do not correspond to any verified data, nor did Martin cite any source to support his figures.
>
> (Haynes, 2014, p. 30)

It was only eight months after first learning about the issue of trafficking from her teenage daughter that actress Jada Pinkett Smith was invited to speak on the topic at the US Senate Foreign Relations Committee (Haynes, 2014). Mira Sorvino, an actress who played an undercover agent in a human trafficking television miniseries, was invited to advise legislators on how to combat human trafficking (Haynes, 2014; Heynen & van der Meulen, 2022).

As with campaigns more broadly, celebrity involvement in anti-trafficking activism is often associated with individualized, quick solutions over long-term, structural changes. Due to the focus on sex trafficking, this includes end-demand policies that discourage men from purchasing sex. For example, in 2009, Ashton Kutcher and Demi Moore started the DNA Foundation, focused on addressing child sex trafficking. In 2011, the "Real Men Don't Buy Girls" campaign began. Videos for the campaign featured numerous celebrities including Drake, Jamie Foxx, Justin Timberlake, Bradley Cooper, Sean Penn, Jason Mraz, Isaiah Mustafa, and Adrian Peterson (Steele & Shores, 2014). But, little additional information about human trafficking was provided during the campaign. In fact, while the campaign website featured a gallery of celebrities,

> information about child and sex slavery were relegated to being the fifth link out of five in the main menu navigation. Clicking that link provided a page with minimal information and instead links to other reports and websites. This information contained little in the way of guiding direct action; the only guidance was to replicate the real man images and to be against buying girls.
>
> (Steele & Shores, 2014, p. 267)

In addition to presenting a narrow picture of trafficking that focuses on female victims and equates sex work with sex trafficking, such campaigns also center on individual responsibility norms over broader structural solutions (Majic, 2018). The cause of trafficking is equating with purchasing sexual services, rather than the larger economic drivers behind entry into prostitution (Majic, 2018).

Charity-based solutions are also popular. In 2011, actress Demi Moore worked with a jeweler to create gold and diamond handcuff necklaces for Valentines Day, with 50% of the proceeds going toward the DNA Foundation (People Staff, 2011). As another example,

> in the online store for the END IT Movement, a prominent anti-trafficking awareness-raising initiative supported by celebrities like Kristen Bell, Ashton Kutcher, and Carrie Underwood, visitors can choose between a range of t-shirts and other paraphernalia (including a onesie for babies) that show their commitment to the cause.
>
> (Heynen & van der Meulen, 2022, pp. 301–302)

Ultimately, many of the campaigns and organizations affiliated with celebrity activism focus only on generating awareness, rather than providing services (Heynen & van der Meulen, 2022).

Consequences

It is important to also examine the impact of these pop culture portrayals. In addition to news media, popular culture also plays a role in shaping public understanding of an issue. For many individuals, such media may be their only source of information about human trafficking (Rodríguez-López, 2018). This includes both feature and documentary films, television episodes, books, campaigns, and celebrity activism. Altogether, these media depictions, including their frequently sensationalized and stereotyped portrayal of the issue, work to become "important sources of information for the public about the realities of trafficking in persons, regardless of the accuracy of facts or authenticity of the narratives captured therein" (Balgamwalla, 2016, p. 13). In addition to shaping awareness among the general public, this media is also seen by criminal justice officials and policymakers. Such media has the potential to perpetuate misrepresentation that then influences human trafficking policy and anti-trafficking responses (Gregoriou & Ras, 2018b). This section explores how media has influenced public knowledge about human trafficking, as well as shaped policing and prosecutorial responses.

Shaping Public Knowledge

For many individuals, news media and popular culture may be their only source of information about human trafficking (Rodríguez-López, 2018). A community survey completed in the Midlands of England found that the most common sources of information about human trafficking included newspapers, the internet, social media, television, and radio (Dando et al., 2016). Surveys completed in Ukraine, Hungary, and Great Britain found that various media sources, and especially television programs, were a primary source of human trafficking knowledge. In Ukraine, the top three sources of knowledge included television news programs, documentaries, and films; in Hungary, the top three included television news programs, newspaper articles, and documentaries; and in Great Britain, the top three categories included television news programs, newspaper articles, and documentaries (Sharapov, 2019).

Various methods have been used to assess the general public's understanding of human trafficking, including large-scale surveys, small focus groups, and vignette studies. Focus groups conducted in Russia in 2007 found narratives that matched the ideal victim of trafficking: "[groups] put together a stereotypical picture of attractive, foolish and naïve girls and women whose level of education was either secondary, lower than secondary or none at all" (Buckley, 2009, p. 238). More recently, focus groups conducted in the UK found that participants associated human trafficking with sexual exploitation, forced prostitution, and illegal migration and were "surprised to learn that people could be forced to work for legitimate businesses like farms and warehouses, rather than directly for organised crime" (Birks & Gardner,

2019, p. 79). A community survey in England found that 89% of respondents believed human trafficking involved illegal smuggling while 58% believed people were trafficked for prostitution (Dando et al., 2016). Similarly, surveys completed in Ukraine, Hungary, and Great Britain found agreement with many human trafficking stereotypes, including that the majority of victims are women trafficked for sexual exploitation that organized crime groups are the primary responsible party for trafficking and support for criminal justice solutions such as tougher border controls and increased criminalization of sex work (Sharapov, 2019).

In the United States, a survey in Pennsylvania found a focus on sex trafficking and prostitution, women and child victims, and the use of kidnapping and force (Strohacker et al., 2023). A nationally representative survey of the United States found that the public held several misconceptions about trafficking, including that "human trafficking victims are almost always female (92%), [trafficking] is another word for smuggling (71%), always requires threats of or actual physical violence (62%), involves mostly illegal immigrants (62%), and requires movement across state or national borders (59%)" (Bouché et al., 2015, p. 30). Another survey found a heightened level of concern for victims who were female, minors, and US citizens (Bouché et al., 2018). Concern does not always translate to support, however, as another nationally representative survey found. While respondents did recognize that immigrants may be more vulnerable to human trafficking, anti-trafficking efforts for that population were not supported (de Vries et al., 2019). This is perhaps due to an association of foreigners as both victims and offenders, equating trafficking with transnational organized crime and general depictions of immigrants as threats to public safety and economic well-being.

Researchers have also examined the impact of believing human trafficking myths, such as equating human trafficking with smuggling and foreigners, associating physical force and bondage with trafficking, and organized crime being behind trafficking operations (Cunningham & Cromer, 2016). Researchers have found gender differences in acceptance of these myths, with men reporting higher acceptance compared to women (Cunningham & Cromer, 2016; Litam et al., 2023). Vignette studies have found that acceptance of these myths is associated with less belief in the situation presented in the vignette and increased victim blaming (Cunningham & Cromer, 2016). Additional vignette studies have found that participants are less likely to accurately identify male victims and labor trafficking victims compared to female and sex trafficking victims, with a lower willingness to help labor trafficking victims compared to sex trafficking victims (Salami et al., 2022).

Many of the films and television episodes reviewed in this chapter emphasized kidnapping and abduction as the primary method used by traffickers, including the 2023 film *Sound of Freedom* which opened with a montage of young children being "snatched" by strangers off the street (Dickson, 2023). These narratives paint a distorted picture of what child trafficking actually looks like. In fact, one nonprofit in Charleston, South Carolina reported that potential volunteers attended a training after seeing *Sound of Freedom* and did not agree with the founder about the realities of sex trafficking, instead arguing back that people were kidnapped and trafficked (Merlan, 2023). In reality, data shows that the vast majority of missing children are runaways. In 2022, 4.4% of cases reported to the National Center for Missing and Exploited Children were family abductions and 0.35% were nonfamily abductions (NCMEC, 2022). So, while abductions can occur in relation to child trafficking, data shows that trafficking connected to endangered runaways and grooming by family and friends is more common. Child victims are likely to be trafficked by someone they know, such as a friend, family member, or romantic partner (Lutnick, 2016). Further, factors like homelessness, a chaotic home life, substance abuse issues, and child welfare or juvenile justice involvement increase children's vulnerability to trafficking (Twis, 2020).

Even individuals involved in anti-trafficking work and organizations present gaps in their knowledge about human trafficking. A study of leaders and staff from 11 community- and faith-based organizations involved in anti-trafficking work in South Los Angeles had high overall knowledge about human trafficking. Still, incorrect answers were frequently given for statements that reflected stereotypes about human trafficking involving physical force and restraint and a requirement to travel across borders to be considered human trafficking (Mobasher et al., 2022).

Influencing Criminal Justice Officials

Beyond the public, criminal justice officials, such as law enforcement officers, prosecutors, judges, and service providers, also fall victim to trafficking stereotypes and use these distorted images of trafficking to make decisions (Austin & Farrell, 2017). In the context of prosecuting trafficking cases, an attorney who was a fellow for the US Department of Justice's anti-trafficking task force emphasized how sensationalized portrayals of trafficking can influence jurors' perceptions: "When you have a case of really subtle coercion that's hard to prove, and the jury is expecting *Taken*, you're not gonna get a conviction" (Dickson, 2023, para.18). Beyond juries, narrow depictions of who is a victim and who is an offender have implications on the practical side of identifying victims and prosecuting cases, as well as implications on what policies get prioritized (Wilson & O'Brien, 2016).

Police knowledge of human trafficking has been shaped by media and popular myths about human trafficking (Farrell et al., 2015). One example of this is found in interviews with Canadian law enforcement working on anti-trafficking task forces. In order to learn about the issue, one officer stated that he read "reports, studies, blogs, internet stuff. Everything I could. 'Pimping' books, breaking down hip hop culture, listening to lyrics, understanding what they're saying. Realizing that it's [knowledge on human trafficking] embedded in popular culture today" (Roots, 2020, p. 101). That same officer noted that he read the book *Somebody's Daughter: Inside the Toronto/Halifax Pimping Ring* by journalist Phonse Jessome, a book which has been noted as blending fact with fiction to make a more melodramatic storyline (Jeffrey & MacDonald, 2011). While training, seminars, and guest speakers can better inform police about the issue of human trafficking, many learn about trafficking through videos or the internet, which may reflect biases about what trafficking looks like (Reis et al., 2022). One survey of local law enforcement in the United States found that only 17% had received any training on human trafficking, while 62% relied on mass media (including the film *Taken*) as their only source to learn about human trafficking (Mapp et al., 2016).

Mass media serving as the primary source of human trafficking information for police means that they are exposed to stereotypical and sensationalized depictions of how trafficking happens, where it happens, who is a victim, and who is an offender. This includes the archetype of the ideal victim. The perpetuation of the ideal victim has influenced law enforcement priorities, emphasizing the sex trafficking of women and girls over male victims, LGBTQ victims, and labor trafficking victims (Todres, 2016). Research shows that law enforcement in the United States has focused on child sex trafficking victims who are US citizens (Balgamwalla, 2016; Farrell & Pfeffer, 2014). One US unit commander explains this focus:

> The blogs and the papers go on about how it's [prostitution] two consenting adults and just a waste of time. But nobody seems to get on their horse when we talk about rescuing kids who are being commercially sexually exploited. So I said, "You know what? That's what we're going to focus on, juvenile prostitution." Under their federal grant, this unit also has the responsibility for investigating sex trafficking cases that involve adults and cases of labor trafficking, but the majority of their cases involve minors.
>
> (Farrell & Pfeffer, 2014, p. 52)

Many human trafficking task forces are located within vice units, leading to a conflation between sex work and sex trafficking. As one Pennsylvania police chief clearly stated: "I consider any form of prostitution human trafficking" (Gibbs et al., 2023, p. 528). Such views influence where law enforcement looks for cases of trafficking. One federal agent stated "I target brothels, because it would be offensive if I knocked on doors looking for domestics … I don't want to go into a worksite without a specific lead" (Peters, 2013, p. 244). It is assumed that brothels are sites of sex trafficking, but the same approach is not used for potential labor trafficking cases.

Such stereotypical views are not limited to US law enforcement either. Police in South Africa conflated human trafficking with prostitution, describing human trafficking as involving young girls in brothels and massage parlors (Morero, 2022). Surveys from Portugal found that police also hold views that reflect an ideal victim, including young, foreign women who are sexually exploited (Cunha et al., 2022). In Australia, state police frequently lumped together trafficking, smuggling, and prostitution (Irwin, 2017). When victims do not reflect this stereotypical portrayal, law enforcement may be reluctant to investigate. One US detective stated that officers were reluctant to investigate cases involving male victims, stating that many "wouldn't touch it" (Farrell & Pfeffer, 2014). Victims who are not young, White, or US citizens may be less likely to be correctly identified as victims (Farrell et al., 2019).

According to the ideal victim archetype, trafficking victims are unable to leave their situation; they are innocent and blameless. Studies have found that law enforcement is more likely to believe victims who have been rescued through their own operations over victims who have fled their trafficking situation on their own (Balgamwalla, 2016). Officers may also not recognize victims when they "do not express gratitude about being 'rescued' by the police" (Farrell et al., 2019). This also includes when victims have drug addictions (Farrell et al., 2019). One detective explained that victims with drug addictions are unreliable and less credible, while a police chief stated "'Ninety-nine-point-nine percent of the time those women are crack whores.' This chief said that he could not justify the expenditure of public resources to investigate their potential victimization" (Farrell et al., 2014, p. 159). Ideas about consent and force are also wrapped up in these perspectives, with law enforcement holding negative perceptions of cases that lack the use of physical force or restraint (Farrell et al., 2014). In reality, there are many ways in which traffickers may exert control over victims, and physical force is just one. Other common tactics of control include psychological abuse, threats, and fraud or deception (CTDC, 2021).

A victim hierarchy is created that separates victims into simplistic categories of good and bad, deserving and undeserving, or slave and migrant (Boukli & Renz, 2019). One researcher describes the hierarchy as ranging from: "'ideal victims' such as young girls abducted from an orphanage and trafficked into prostitution, down to women already working in the sex industry who are persuaded that the money could be better if they migrate to another country, and then find themselves trapped in unacceptable conditions or in debt bondage" (Hoyle et al., 2011, p. 315). This hierarchy can result in some victims being offered less, or even no support, compared to those ideal victims (Gregoriou & Ras, 2018b; Jones & Kingshott, 2016). Research shows that criminal justice personnel may also be less sympathetic or more reluctant to treat someone as a victim if they do not fit the ideal victim construction (Farrell et al., 2010, 2014).

As with pop culture portrayals, law enforcement also frequently emphasized the ties between organized crime and trafficking. A survey conducted by municipal and county police departments in the United States found that 75% of respondents agreed that transnational organized crime groups were responsible for human trafficking (Wilson et al., 2006). Portuguese police also reporting believing that traffickers are integrated into organized crime networks (Cunha et al., 2022). One Canadian officer even estimated that 85–90% of trafficking activities involved organized crime, despite a lack of data to substantiate such strong connections (Roots, 2020).

Prosecutors and judges are also influenced by media portrayals of human trafficking. Reflecting many facets of the ideal victim, one study of US federal cases found that sex trafficking cases involving US citizens, minors, and high rates of violence made up the majority of prosecutions (Farrell et al., 2014). Magistrates in Portugal also repeated similar misconceptions, such as believing human trafficking always involves physical force against the victim and that traffickers are usually strangers to their victims (Lourenço et al., 2019). An interview with a US state prosecutor reflects on how these biases impact cases:

> One prosecutor described how he lost a sex trafficking case involving a victim who was a U.S. citizen when a judge allowed the defense attorney to claim that trafficking only happens to immigrants smuggled across borders (which is not required by the law). Although the prosecutor objected, he believed that the judge's action biased the jury's decision toward acquittal.
>
> (Farrell et al., 2014, p. 153)

Ultimately, such narrow views of human trafficking divert resources from labor trafficking and lead to an under-identification of legitimate victims (Wilson & O'Brien, 2016). Migrants and sex workers experiencing exploitation often face criminalization rather than receive help (Boggiani, 2015; Wilson & O'Brien, 2016). Further, the media's framing of the issue of human trafficking as primarily a crime and justice problem obscures the structural factors that leave individuals vulnerable to trafficking in the first place. By using a simplified victim and villain narrative, human trafficking is reduced to an individual problem remedied by law enforcement and charity (Raby & Chazal, 2022). This isolation overlooks the complex role that factors like poverty, discrimination, and demand for cheap labor all play (Albright & D'Adamo, 2017; Gregoriou & Ras, 2018b).

5 The Sporting Event Panic

This chapter explores media coverage of event-centered panics. Frequently, large sporting events have been touted as hot spots for trafficking, despite little evidence to support such claims. These panics highlight conflation between sex work and sex trafficking, as well as differences in how labor trafficking is covered by the media. This chapter also explores the consequences of these panics, including increased harassment of sex workers, the use of raids and rescues, and the arrest-to-assist model applied to trafficking victims.

Trafficking at Mega-Events

While mega-events may take on multiple definitions, the following sociological perspective on mega-events is most applicable here. Roche (2000, p. 1) defines mega-events as "large-scale cultural (including commercial and sporting) events which have a dramatic character, mass popular appeal and international significance." The claim that sex trafficking increases at such events is tied to the belief that large groups of foreign men attend such events without their significant others, leading to an increase in demand for paid sexual services, which traffickers respond to in order to increase their profits (Boecking et al., 2019; Ham, 2011; Weitzer, 2014). This perspective was reflected in a 2006 European Parliament resolution on forced prostitution at world sporting events which boldly stated "experience has shown that any major sporting event at which large numbers of people congregate results in a temporary and spectacular increase in the demand for sexual services" (European Parliament, 2006, para.C). These claims have been repeated by prostitution abolitionist groups, politicians, and journalists, with estimated figures of victims ranging from 10,000 to 100,000 at each event (Ham, 2011; Weitzer, 2014).

This is despite a lack of evidence to support such figures. For example, a study using official police data from the month before, during, and after the 2018 Formula 1 Grand Prix in Austin, Texas found no statistically significant increases in violent crimes, property crimes, sex crimes, and human trafficking (Piquero et al., 2021). While not all crimes may be reported to the police,

DOI: 10.4324/9781003439004-5

the authors note there was no increase in human trafficking despite increased law enforcement focus on the issue. Studies have also debunked the idea that it is cost-effective for traffickers to move victims into a city for such short-term events (Weitzer, 2014). One police inspector even stated in relation to the 2010 Olympic games that "It costs a lot of money to move people around. It's a short-term event, so from a trafficker's perspective, it wouldn't make a lot of sense" (Ham, 2011, p. 18). In addition to facing significant empirical issues and biased data from law enforcement, many studies conducted on the relationship between sex trafficking and sporting events often conflate sex work with trafficking (Boecking et al., 2019; Matheson & Finkel, 2013). Ultimately, there have been few well-designed empirical studies on the topic, making it difficult to accurately assess and estimate the relationship between such events and trafficking (Finkel & Finkel, 2015).

If there is such a lack of evidence, why does this claim continue to reappear in the media during such events? One scholar suggests that the claim is useful for fundraising, with dramatic claims grabbing the public's attention and such campaigns providing an easy way to "do something" (Ham, 2011). By cultivating a moral panic, such claims also work to justify crackdowns on migrants and sex workers, as will be explored in more depth later in this chapter. Such social control measures include the criminalization and harassment of sex workers and migrants while ignoring the real connections between these events and other human rights violations. Further, the awareness campaigns around such events tend to be sensationalized and based on exaggerated numbers. They present a very narrow image of what trafficking and trafficking victims look like and divert resources from services for trafficked persons (Ham, 2011; Martin & Hill, 2017). The next several sections take a closer look at some of the mega-events frequently tied to trafficking, including the Olympics, World Cup, and Super Bowl.

The Olympics

The first documented concerns about mega-sporting events and sex trafficking originated with the 2004 Olympics in Athens, Greece (Martin & Hill, 2017). Prior to the event, an Italian NGO remarked that traffickers were likely to bring in more women to meet an expected increase in demand (Hennig et al., 2007). Following the event, some have repeated a statistic that trafficking increased by 95% during this event. This number comes from an increase in the yearly total number of identified victims in Greece, from 93 reported victims in 2003 to 181 reported victims in 2004. However, none of the identified victims from 2004 were linked to the Olympic Games, suggesting instead that improvements in detection and reporting efforts led to the increase (Ham, 2011). While prostitution is legal in Greece, China hosted the 2008 Olympics, where prostitution is criminalized. Still, no link was found between sex trafficking and the sporting event (Hayes, 2010).

As stated previously, the myth of trafficking at such events is perhaps perpetuated because it is a strong platform for fundraising and campaigning. NGOs can leverage their visibility during such events to promote their anti-trafficking campaigns (De Shalit, 2014). In the lead-up to the 2010 Olympics in Vancouver, Canada a newspaper reported the event was viewed as "the biggest opportunity for [the Salvation Army] in decades… [they are] set to launch a huge campaign" (Wallace, 2010, para.9). As such, in the fall of 2008 in Vancouver, the Salvation Army launched "The Truth Isn't Sexy" which included ads on billboards, in transit shelters, and men's bathrooms. The graphic and sensationalist ads featured young women being brutalized by pimps and traffickers. As one local sex worker stated of the ads: "having a billboard of an underage girl in her underwear being stomped on can be triggering; it's very graphic. It's selling sex and violence to prevent them. The posters themselves were actually very titillating in the imagery that they used" (Lepp, 2013, p. 263). The educational aspect and effectiveness of such ads have been criticized, with some pointing out that they focus on presenting disturbing situations or misleading information solely to evoke an emotional response. This includes portraying a very narrow view of who is a trafficking victim (women and girls) and what trafficking looks like (physical violence and kidnapping for the purpose of sex) (Matheson & Finkel, 2013).

A study with 230 sex workers conducted by the Global Alliance Against Traffic in Women found that demand actually decreased during the Olympic games (Ham, 2011). Similarly, another study found no increases in reports of new, youthful, or trafficked sex workers during the 2010 Olympics (Deering et al., 2012). Instead of increases in trafficking, studies have found that measures taken in the name of anti-trafficking efforts instead harmed sex workers. A study of ten Olympic host cities found that police crackdowns, raids, and arrests related to sex work have not identified trafficking victims, but instead resulted in the harassment of sex workers and increased fear and distrust of police (Bowen & Shannon Frontline Consulting, 2009). In the lead-up to the 2012 Olympics in London, England, police conducted several raids on brothels, with only an estimated 1% success rate of finding trafficking victims. Specifically, after 822 raids, only 11 genuine victims of trafficking were identified (Boff, 2012). Instead, the forcible removal of sex workers from an area increased their isolation, making them more vulnerable to violence from clients and disrupting their access to health and safety services (Deering & Shannon, 2012).

The World Cup

Just as the 2004 Olympics was a catalyst for creating a purported link between sex trafficking and sporting events, so was the 2006 World Cup in Germany. Inter-governmental discussions prior to the World Cup on this issue were perhaps jumped upon due to Germany's policy toward sex work. More specifically, the Swedish government claimed that the German policy of legalized prostitution would further increase the risk of sex trafficking at the World Cup (Ham, 2011). Likewise, the United States used the opportunity to lobby for the criminalization of sex work in Germany (Ham, 2011; Hayes, 2010). In fact, the US House of Representatives' Subcommittee on Africa, Global Human Rights and International Operations held a hearing that was titled "Germany's World Cup Brothels: 40,000 Women and Children at Risk of Exploitation through Trafficking," which was used to criticize Germany's prostitution policy. In a gross misrepresentation of German law that conflated prostitution with trafficking, Congressman Christopher H. Smith argued that "since the matches were being held in Germany, which legalized pimping and prostitution in 2001—that World Cup fans would be legally free to rape women in brothels or even in mobile units designed specifically for this form of exploitation" (Germany's World Cup Brothels, 2006). Similar discussions occurred with the 2004 Olympics due to the Greek government's policy on regulating prostitution (Ham, 2011).

As in other human trafficking panics, abolitionist feminist groups, conservatives, and faith-based organizations used the opportunity to push for criminalization of sex work (Hayes, 2010). For example, Stop the Traffick, which embraces an anti-prostitution stance, campaigned around the 2010 World Cup. Their website presented several nonfactual and unsubstantiated claims, including that "the legalization of sex work makes trafficking worse, that Germany and Australia regret legalizing sex work, and that sex work and trafficking are the same thing" (Gould, 2010, p. 38). Ultimately, these events highlight a longstanding tension between anti-trafficking groups that view prostitution and consensual sex work as distinct from human trafficking and those that do not.

One of the more common statistics repeated by journalists, politicians, and organizations is that 40,000 women and girls are trafficked at each World Cup (Mitchell, 2022). The figure seems to have originated in connection to the 2006 World Cup, though it was stated as an estimate of the number of migrant sex workers expected to arrive in Germany (Milivojević & Pickering, 2008). The figure quickly shifted from an estimate of prostitutes to an estimate of trafficking victims (Bonthuys, 2012). As a "zombie statistic," the 40,000 estimate was repeated and recycled by media at future events (Mitchell, 2022). This includes the 2010 World Cup in South Africa, with even the South African Central Drug Authority claiming that 40,000 women would be "imported" for the event (Delva et al., 2011; Ham, 2011).

Multiple analyses of news reports leading up to the 2010 World Cup in South Africa found a narrow portrayal of trafficking that reflected stereotypes about victims and offenders alike (Bonthuys, 2012; Francis & Emser, 2014). Beyond concerns about an increase in the trafficking of women for sex, there were fears that children would be kidnapped and sold into sexual slavery as well. These themes are reflected in the images from the It's a Penalty

Campaign for the 2014 World Cup in Brazil. Juxtaposed against the forlorn face of a young Black child, one of their ads reads "Young children on the streets of Brazil have no one to protect them against potential traffickers." Another shows the face of a very young White girl holding a baby doll, the text overlay stating "Did you know street children in Brazil, without homes or family, are often captured and sold as sex slaves?" Religious organizations reflected similar sentiments, with one secretary stating to a news outlet about the 2006 World Cup in Germany:

> We are very anxious about what will happen in Germany next month. The stories of these girls locked in houses are absolutely horrendous. These young women are either sold by their families, kidnapped or believe they are going to decent jobs to earn money to send home. They end up without any rights and with ruined lives.
>
> (Morgan, 2006, para.7)

Traffickers were described as foreigners, with Nigerian crime syndicates reportedly taking advantage of "porous borders" (Bonthuys, 2012; Francis & Emser, 2014; Ham, 2011). UNICEF's Red Card campaign claimed that more than 500 criminal gangs were involved in the sex trade in South Africa prior to the 2010 World Cup (Gould, 2010).

Instead, studies have found that few trafficking victims are identified at these events, even with increased law enforcement and public awareness. This includes a significant lack of evidence that trafficking increased during the 2006 World Cup in Germany, with residents surveyed also having no perceived increases in sex work (Bonthuys, 2012). The government reported no cases of trafficking during the 2010 World Cup in South Africa (Ham, 2011; South African Police Service, 2011). Further, there was no evidence of a significant spike in sex work or foreign sex workers migrating to the area for the event (Delva et al., 2011; Richter et al., 2012; Richter & Delva, 2011). Contrary to the idea that soccer fans are driving demand and exploitation of women, research has shown that some sex workers saw foreigners as easy marks: "Rather than clients exploiting prostitutes, prostitutes routinely described how easy it was to rob, pickpocket, bamboozle, and even beat up and mug clients during major sporting events" (Mitchell, 2022, p. 98). Similar to the Olympics, the real danger includes the intimidation and harassment of sex workers by police. Irina Maslova, a sex worker rights activist, reported that at the 2018 World Cup in Russia, sex workers were held by police without clothes, rounded up with other undesirable populations, and concentrated in camps outside the city (Mitchell, 2022). As one anti-trafficking organization in Germany reported: "Police raided 71 brothels in Berlin during the 2006 World Cup. Police found no evidence of trafficking but deported ten women" (Ham, 2011, p. 21). Ultimately, as with the Olympics, the panic did not bear out in reality. In addition to the negative treatment of sex workers, anti-trafficking organizations report that the hyperbolic claims and sensationalized campaigns may actually make anti-trafficking work more difficult. With the hype around the statistic of 40,000 women being trafficked failing to come true, anti-trafficking organizations may have more difficulty garnering attention and believability in the future (Hennig et al., 2007). Further, with panics focused around such short-term events and coverage of the issue of trafficking disappearing immediately following the event, generating support for long-term services for victims is also made more complicated (Ham, 2011).

The Super Bowl

While the Super Bowl is not an international sporting event, it is one of the largest annual sporting events in the United States, and as such, has also been connected with sex trafficking. Journalists, politicians, and organizations repeat the claim yearly, with estimates ranging from 10,000 to 100,000 at each Super Bowl (Ham, 2011). In their 2023 Super Bowl Impact Report, the organization It's a Penalty claimed that their sporting event campaigns have "facilitated the protection of 17,000 survivors of abuse, exploitation and human trafficking,* as well as potentially prevented thousands more from being victimised" (It's a Penalty, 2023, p. 3). Reading the small print at the bottom for the asterisk denotes that the 17,000 survivors are only an estimated figure that includes *potential* media reach and social media views. In a press release, Senator Amy Klobuchar claims that the Super Bowl "has become one of the largest venues for sex trafficking in the country" (Klobuchar, 2014, para.4). Texas Attorney General Greg Abbott stated that "The Super Bowl is the greatest show on Earth, but it also has an ugly underbelly… It's commonly known as the single largest human trafficking incident in the United States" and linked the event to international sex trafficking rings (Jervis, 2011, para.4). One study found that an alarming 76% of US print media between 2010 and 2016 repeated the myth of sex trafficking at the Super Bowl (Martin & Hill, 2019). These articles used sensationalist language, focused on the use of stings and increased policing of sex workers, and often conflated prostitution arrests with trafficking.

There have been few studies that have empirically assessed the link between sex trafficking and the Super Bowl. Instead, many studies have used online sexual service advertisements to assess the connection. However, findings from studies such as these should be viewed with caution. There is the conflation between sex work and sex trafficking when using advertisements as a measure of the relationship between the Super Bowl and trafficking. For example, one study of the 2020 and 2021 Super Bowls claimed to find an increase in online advertisements that exhibit indicators of sex trafficking. These indicators include things such as multiple advertisements using the same phone number, text indicating private and undisclosed locations, short stays, and offerings of certain types of sexual services (Huang et al.,

2022). Another study of the 2014, 2015, and 2016 Super Bowls took a similar approach, flagging advertisements as potential trafficked minors if the ad contained youthful descriptors, images contained youthful room décor, and youthful faces and poses (Roe-Sepowitz et al., 2015). Such indicators cannot definitively be used as evidence of a relationship between sex trafficking and the Super Bowl and may instead relate to the criminalized nature of sex work in the United States. Further, additional analysis has shown that the Super Bowl is not unique in increase of sex advertisements. Beyond sporting events, festivals, conventions, and other large events have also shown increases in the number of advertisements (Boecking et al., 2019; Miller et al., 2016).

A common response to the claims that sex trafficking increases in the host city of the Super Bowl has been to increase policing efforts. As with the Olympics and the World Cup, this has resulted in a pattern of sex workers being arrested, harassed, and further stigmatized (Martin & Hill, 2017). Campaigns have also fallen into stereotypical portrayals of human trafficking, with one campaign image showing a distressed young girl with duct tape over her mouth (Sant et al., 2023). As Mitchell (2022, p. 226) concludes about sporting events and moral panics:

> [Moral entrepreneurs] rely on melodramatic narratives and the manufacture of perfect victims as they chase after funding and celebrity sponsorship. But all the smoke and mirrors of "awareness raising" have taught society to be constantly vigilant for any sign of sex trafficking, always in a state of hyperawareness and fear. This constant panic has consequences for marginalized groups such as sex workers, especially the lower-class and non-white ones, who are then made more susceptible to police violence, state surveillance, and carceral systems.

For example, the organization It's a Penalty campaigns around major sporting events, including the Olympics, World Cups, and Super Bowls. A common strategy has been to make use of celebrities and athletes in their campaigns in order to teach the public to "know the signs" of trafficking and report their suspicions (Sant et al., 2023). While awareness is important, such campaigns can encourage a "paranoid reading of strangers" and a suspicion of women, minorities, and foreigners (Mitchell, 2022). Calling the cops then leads to harassment and even arrest for such populations. Studies have noted that arrest and/or harassment by police is more likely if the individual does not fit the stereotypical portrait of a "victim" (Martin & Hill, 2017). In the United States, where sex work is criminalized, a criminal record for prostitution carries "long-term negative consequences" including stigmatization and reduced access to employment and housing (Martin & Hill, 2017).

Raids and Rescues

The panic around mega-sporting events has emphasized sex trafficking. Campaigns present stereotypical notions of trafficking that reflect an ideal victim—a young girl who has fallen prey to sex traffickers and is in need of rescue (Martin & Hill, 2017). The solutions proposed, however, end up penalizing both trafficking victims and sex workers, leading to their harassment, arrest, and even deportation (Ham, 2011).

Specifically, law enforcement has often used the practice of raids as the primary method to identify and "rescue" trafficking victims (Ham, 2011). In the run-up to mega-sporting events, anti-trafficking raids take place, with names like Operation Shangri-la in Brazil prior to the World Cup, Operation Pentameter in London prior to the Olympics, and Operation Super Bowl in New York. These raids result in arrests of clients and women that make the news, though many times after they are released or deported due to a lack of evidence of trafficking (Boff, 2012; Mitchell, 2016; Musto, 2016). These raids may result in sex workers experiencing horrific violence at the hands of police as the two excerpts from sex workers in Brazil and South Africa demonstrate:

> On May 23, 2014, police entered the house where three hundred women were legally selling sex in Niteroi, Rio de Janeiro. Acting without a court order, the police stole the women's money, extorted them, and singled several of the women out for rape. Isabel was one of the women whom police beat and gang- raped in this operation that occurred just weeks before the World Cup. When police were done, they closed the building and labeled the rooms as crime scenes. Unlike the other women who were intimidated by police, Isabel pressed her claim and testified against them. On June 21, men abducted her and tortured her by cutting her with razor blades all over her body. They showed her pictures of her children and told her to stop talking to the press. Isabel went from making US$4,000 a month selling sex legally to being totally destitute and homeless.
>
> (Mitchell, 2016, p. 343)

> "Police arrest sex workers and take our money. They sleep with us and they don't pay. They take clients' money and pepper spray our vaginas and clients' penises" - Female sex worker, Johannesburg.
>
> (Richter & Delva, 2011, p. 25)

Such raids have not proven to be a highly successful method of identifying trafficking victims. Instead, they are likely to increase sex workers vulnerability and exposure to violence as their work is driven further underground, while also creating a climate of fear and distrust with the authorities.

The use of raid and rescue is not limited to mega-sporting events. This practice has become widespread globally as a primary method to identify and assist trafficking victims. Raids in Indonesia and India have also been noted as subjecting sex workers to physical and sexual abuse by police (Ahmed & Seshu, 2012). In the United States, women reported that police raids were chaotic and traumatic events (Ditmore & Thukral, 2012). One woman, arrested seven times and never screened for trafficking, stated of raids:

> They … bang on the door, they break the door, they come in with the guns out! ... It's really horrible, sometimes if they are very angry, they don't let you get dressed … One never lets go of the fear. Being afraid never goes away. They provoke that.
>
> (Ditmore, 2009, p. 16)

Ultimately, many sex workers fear raids due to the harms and trauma that occur both during and after the raids, including interrogation, arrest and detention, prosecution, and even deportation (Hill, 2016).

Under the rescue narrative, individuals will react to their "rescue" with gratitude, cooperate with police, and be appreciative of social services provided to them. In reality, both sex workers and trafficking victims may react in a variety of ways, with exiting the sex industry being a complex process (Martin & Hill, 2017). There are a variety of reasons an individual may choose to engage in sex work, including economic and social pressures. Many enter sex work knowingly due to the earning potential it offers (Gould, 2010; Zhang, 2010). Barriers to leaving sex work may include housing, employment, and educational opportunities (Marcus et al., 2014). There is a lack of nuance when women are portrayed as either calculating migrant sex workers undeserving of help or as naïve and innocent trafficking victims (Mahdavi, 2011). While sex workers may report dissatisfaction with pay and working conditions, not every sex worker is a trafficking victim forced or coerced into the sex industry (Mai, 2013). One lawyer states that to conflate the two is a disservice to trafficking victims, noting:

> I also have many, many friends and clients, and allies, that engage voluntarily in sex work. So if I'm going to contrast a Ph.D. student who is escorting out of her home twice a week to make ends meet, with somebody who at 16, is being brutally raped and forced to stay out on the street all night, it's really demeaning and horrific to both of them to say 'you're experiencing the same thing,' or, 'we can put you under the same rubric of trafficking.' It's incredibly belittling to both of their experiences of what they're doing. And it removes agency from both of them, really, by denying their own experience of what they're going through.
>
> (Jackson, 2016, p. 37)

Frequently, women and girls who have been "rescued" through these operations are then placed in public or private shelters. These shelters may be open, where the rights of victims are respected and they are free to come and go while receiving support and services, or closed, where victims are "effectively imprisoned" (Gallagher & Pearson, 2010). In a closed shelter, there is control over who individuals may speak to, where they are able to go, and how long they must remain there. Victims may be held for months or years as their case moves slowly through the court system. Closed shelters have been used around the world, including countries such as Russia, Thailand, Nigeria, and India. In Malaysia, shelter detention is used for both foreign and domestic victims of trafficking—escaping from the shelter only increases the length of your detention and it is considered a crime to help someone escape (Gallagher & Pearson, 2010). In Thailand, women held in shelters reported intrusive and nonconsensual medical tests, including vaginal examinations, monitoring of mail and phone calls, prohibited contact with outsiders, and punishments if rules were not followed (Empower Foundation, 2012).

The campaigns and discourse around trafficking at these events also reflect racialized and anti-immigrant sentiments (Martin & Hill, 2017). Trafficking is portrayed as a transnational problem, connected with immigration, foreign traffickers and victims, and international crime rings. Law enforcement and NGOs may target specific racial or ethnic groups based on stereotypes of both trafficked women and traffickers (Ham, 2011; Shih, 2016). Altogether this culminates in the policing of women's movement. Anti-trafficking measures put in place in relation to the 2006 World Cup impacted not only sex workers but also foreign women visiting Germany for the event (Milivojević & Pickering, 2008). An open border between Nepal and India has historically involved free movement. While men's movement still occurs as an accepted practice, women's movement across this border is now heavily policed in the name of "rescuing" them from trafficking. This includes "border guards" employed by a NGO focused on rescue forcibly returning women and girls to their villages or placing them in shelters (Lee, 2014).

Labor Trafficking

While significant media attention has focused on these mega-events and sex trafficking, less coverage has been devoted to their links with labor exploitation and labor trafficking. To host the Olympics or World Cup, nations regularly invest billions in building infrastructure for the event (Bowersox, 2016). This includes expanding stadium capacities, building new venues and training grounds, and additional facilities, often in a relatively short time period (Al Thani, 2021). For the 2008 Olympics in Beijing, China constructed 19 new structures and renovated 13 existing ones (Anderson, 2015). Rushing to complete these projects and working to cut costs has resulted in the exploitation and trafficking of migrant laborers (Bowersox, 2016).

For example, almost 100,000 workers migrated to the area near Sochi, Russia to work in projects related to the 2014 Winter Olympics. These conditions of these workers included little to no pay, excessive working hours with few days off, and confiscation of passports and work permits as companies "failed to abide by labor and human trafficking laws" (Anderson, 2015, p. 44). In addition to these abuses, interviews with migrant workers from Armenia, Kyrgyzstan, Serbia, Tajikistan, Ukraine, and Uzbekistan also documented lack of employment contracts, failure to follow the terms of a contract, physical and psychological abuse, overcrowded employer-provided housing, and inadequate employer-provided meals (Buchanan, 2013). One worker from Serbia stated of the situation: "The situation was bad because they weren't paying regular wages or any real money at all. But I couldn't do anything because they had my passport and I had no money. I had no choice but to just keep working" (Buchanan, 2013, p. 38). Migrant workers faced similar conditions in China leading up to the 2008 Olympics in Beijing, including improper pay deductions, unpaid overtime, and substandard living conditions (Richardson, 2008). At the most extreme end, workers have died as a result of the dire working conditions. Surrounding the 2004 Olympics in Greece are the deaths of 13 Greeks and at least 25 undocumented migrant workers (Ham, 2011).

More recently, half a million mostly foreign construction workers were involved in building nine stadiums and other infrastructure for the 2022 World Cup in Qatar (Mitchell, 2022). Officially, only 400 to 500 migrant worker deaths have been confirmed, though there is evidence that places the more accurate number in the several thousands. Qatar has recorded over 15,000 non-nationals deaths between 2010 and 2019, but without a breakdown in the data and given the government's failure to meaningfully investigate deaths on the construction sites, the true statistic may never be known (Page & Worden, 2022). With a population of only around 2.5 million, Qatar required migrant labor to complete the construction necessary to host the World Cup (Christenson, 2018). The migrant sponsorship system used in Qatar contributes to situations of abuse and exploitation. Known as the Kafala system, migrants are tied to their sponsor for employment. Their continued residence and ability to work in Qatar are dependent on this sponsor, and this relationship can leave workers vulnerable to exploitative situations (Mahdavi, 2011). Attempts to reform the system have not resulted in significant changes, and under the new law, "workers remain within their employer's control and may not, without their employer's permission, change jobs during contracted periods. Additionally, exit permits are still required, and employers can block employees from getting these permits" (Christenson, 2018, p. 97).

Labor exploitation and trafficking also occur in relation to the consumer goods that are produced for these events, including commemorative sportswear and souvenirs. A study of licensed goods produced by four companies for the 2008 Olympics in Beijing found "appalling disregard for their workers' health and for local labour laws and regulations in the following areas: working hours, pay scale; the hiring of minors and children; and health and safety conditions" (Play Fair, 2007, p. 5). For example, one company required labor of over 13 hours a day, 7 days a week with pay falling 50% below the legal minimum.

It is not only labor exploitation that occurs in relation to mega-sporting events either, as research has shown the violation of other human rights as well. A report from the Human Rights Watch noted five major human rights abuses associated with these events, including forced evictions; abuse and exploitation of migrant workers; silencing of activists; threats, intimidation, and arrests of journalists; and discrimination (Worden, 2015). Forced evictions were used widely in Brazil leading up to the 2016 Olympic Games in Rio de Janeiro, with close to 80,000 individuals evicted across the city between 2009 and 2015 (Talbot & Carter, 2018). One community was reduced from around 600 families to just 20, with their homes destroyed (Talbot & Carter, 2018). In South Africa, 10,000 locals were evicted leading up to the 2010 World Cup (Al Thani, 2021). Forcible evictions also occurred in relation to the 2014 Winter Olympics in Sochi, Russia, in addition to a crackdown on journalists and anti-LGBT discrimination (Worden, 2015). Foreign journalists who attempted to report on the migrant working conditions in Qatar related to the 2022 World Cup were jailed, with their equipment seized and evidence destroyed (Mitchell, 2022).

Ultimately, the media panic around mega-sporting events and sex trafficking has little supporting evidence. Instead, the claims and rumors have been used to generate campaigns and funding. The rescue narrative is attractive because donors are fed numbers on arrests as a quick and measurable outcome, with the reliable concept of a "hero, victim, and villain" (Jones et al., 2018). The resources devoted by governments and organizations to eliminating this rumored problem could have been directed toward other needs that address the underlying vulnerabilities connected to both sex work and sex trafficking. This includes long-term services and resources that respect the rights of individuals and recognize that their path may be a messy one. As one staff member of an NGO in Thailand stated of the rescue industry: "You may rescue them, give them a vocation like hairdressing. They go back to their country of origin, there is no hairdressing salon. What happens? They go back into the trade, in another area" (Jones et al., 2018, p. 246).

6 The Social Media Panic

This chapter examines the ways that modern technology, and specifically social media, shape human trafficking panics. This includes the use of hashtags and online social movements in generating misinformation, as well as the role of the internet in human trafficking, and how legislation is trying to tackle the issue. Broadly, media includes television, music, movies, newspapers, and online media accessible via phones and laptops, all of which cultural criminology can be used to analyze (Ferrell, 1999). Social media can be defined as referring to a "medium wherein 'ordinary' people in ordinary social networks (as opposed to professional journalists) can create user-generated 'news' (in a broadly defined sense… This new medium is designed to facilitate social interaction, the sharing of digital media, and collaboration)" (Murthy, 2012, p. 1061). This includes websites like Facebook, Twitter, and Instagram which act as both means of personal interconnection and means of information seeking. Through the use of "hashtags and search terms [users can comb through] libraries of user-produced content, often accessing real-time information on emerging events" (Moran et al., 2023, p. 4). Social media allows for news about human trafficking, including misinformation and conspiracies, to quickly spread.

Conspiracy theories can be taken as a pejorative term that refers to

> conspiracy-based explanations which deal with large scale, dramatic social and political events … for explanations that do not just describe or explain an alleged conspiracy, but also *uncover* it and in doing so expose some remarkable and hitherto unknown 'truth' about the world.
>
> (Byford, 2011, p. 21)

Several defining features of conspiracies include seeing things as black and white without nuance, it is simply good versus evil, and establishing themselves as irrefutable, any evidence that contradicts the conspiracy is simply evidence of the conspiring itself (Byford, 2011). This frequently includes dismissing any individuals or organizations speaking out against the conspiracy as part of "mainstream media" or the "deep state" (Watson, 2023).

DOI: 10.4324/9781003439004-6

These features are reflected in many trafficking conspiracies that have spread through social media in the last decade. Echo chambers, where individuals are not exposed to differing opinions, and filter bubbles, where search algorithms predict what information users prefer to see, serve to perpetuate these conspiracies throughout social media (Prakash et al., 2022).

In many ways, social media has enabled the spread of human trafficking conspiracies. This includes allowing for panic and hysteria to endure. In the 1980s, the missing children panic centered around strangers abducting and killing children. But a Pulitzer Prize-winning news story and a two-part PBS special debunking the panic allowed for accurate information to reach individuals and the panic faded away (Tiffany, 2021). Today's panic about child sex trafficking reflects many of these fears again, though social media allows for the panic to remain sustained. Tiffany (2021, para.12) summarizes the role of social media as such

> On Facebook and Instagram, friends and neighbors share unsettling statistics and dire images in formats designed for online communities that reward displays of concern. Because today's messaging about child sex trafficking is so decentralized and fluid, it is impervious to gatekeepers who would knock down its most outlandish claims. The phenomenon suggests the possibility of a new law of social-media physics: A panic in motion can stay in motion.

Social media presents individuals with new forms of communication, information sharing, and knowledge seeking. Further, the lack of accurate information and data on human trafficking generally allows for conspiracies to more easily take hold (Moran et al., 2023).

Hashtags and Online Movements

#QAnon

QAnon originated on the forum website 4chan, which allows users to post anonymously. On October 28, 2017 "Q" began posting cryptic messages claiming to be a US intelligence official with knowledge of a secret "global cabal" that then-President Trump was fighting. QAnon claims the cabal included government officials involved in human trafficking, covering it up and preventing enforcement of anti-trafficking laws (Uscinski & Enders, 2023). The messaging associated with QAnon spread to other social media sites, such as Facebook, Instagram, Twitter, YouTube, and Discord (Boettcher, 2022). The message that children are being sexually abused and must be saved can become a strong motive for people to act, and in 2019, the FBI labeled the QAnon conspiracy as a domestic terror threat (Rajan et al., 2021).

A QAnon crime map from the University of Maryland (2023) indicates that QAnon supporters are implicated in over 130 violent criminal acts between 2016 and 2023 across 11 different countries: the United States, the Netherlands, Canada, Australia, Germany, France, the United Kingdom, New Zealand, Japan, Switzerland, and Croatia. These crimes include "kidnappings related to custody issues, weapons offenses, assault, murder, arson, and terrorism" (Benton & Peterka-Benton, 2021, p. 125). For one case, this includes a QAnon supporter in Texas crashing into another car while drunk, claiming that she was rescuing a young girl from being trafficked by the driver who she claimed was a pedophile (Boettcher, 2022).

Over 130 various anti-trafficking organizations in the United States have issued an open letter noting the harm that QAnon conspiracy claims perpetuate in regard to anti-trafficking work (Watson, 2023). Despite this, anti-trafficking advocates and the voices of survivors themselves have been largely ignored. In US politics, two vocal QAnon supporters, Majorie Taylor Green (Georgia) and Lauren Boebert (Colorado), were elected to Congress in the 2020 election, with 73 candidates endorsing or promoting QAnon content running in 2022 (Kaplan, 2021).

Widespread belief in QAnon has remained relatively low and stable over time according to polling in the United States, though several core tenets of the conspiracy have garnered more widespread belief. One national survey found that 50% of Americans think that the number of trafficked children is 300,000 or higher and 35% agree with the statement that "elites, from government and Hollywood, are engaged in a massive child sex trafficking racket" (Uscinski & Enders, 2021). Increasing acceptance of such beliefs shapes widespread perceptions of human trafficking and makes it difficult for anti-trafficking advocates to get accurate information out.

Ultimately, QAnon has reified many of the old tropes about human trafficking. This includes centering White women and children supposedly at risk of being kidnapped and sold into sexual slavery, and a simplified portrayal that involves an innocent victim, an evil offender, and a good rescuer (Boettcher, 2022). Further demonstrating similarities to the early White slave panic, these trafficking conspiracies are constructed in relation to threats to the traditional moral order. This includes "paranoia about LGBTQ+ rights, perceptions of politically radical enemies, and fears about losing a privileged white status [which] permeate the ideology of many Q believers" (Benton & Peterka-Benton, 2021, p. 122). In fact, research has found that QAnon-related imagery overrepresents young White children compared to the actual demographics of child trafficking victims (Buntain et al., 2022). Further, legitimate concerns about child abuse and human trafficking, along with notable pedophilia and #metoo scandals across several countries work to enhance individual susceptibility to QAnon-related conspiracies (Goldenberg et al., 2021). It is this idea that women and children are being abducted and forced into prostitution that has gone on to be reflected in many adjacent offshoots of QAnon, including Pizzagate, Wayfairgate, and Save the Children.

#Pizzagate, #Wayfairgate, and #SaveTheChildren

The Pizzagate conspiracy alleged that coded words and symbols were found in emails related to Hillary Clinton's 2016 Presidential campaign, where pizza-related terms referenced an international child sex ring. These signs supposedly pointed to Comet Ping Pong, a pizzeria in Washington DC where conspiracists alleged child trafficking victims were held in a basement. On December 4, 2016, a young man traveled from North Carolina to the restaurant where he opened fire with an AR-15 with the aim of saving the children (Benton & Peterka-Benton, 2021). Fortunately, no individual was hurt in this incident, but it demonstrates how quickly these conspiracies may lead to action taken offline. While Pizzagate preceded QAnon, it was quickly incorporated into the wider narrative focused on making connections between child sex trafficking and "the deep state."

On July 10, 2020, a hashtag appeared and quickly went viral across various social media platforms. #WayfairGate and its associated hashtags, such as #wayfairchildtrafficking and #wayfairconspiracy, rapidly spread. Wayfairgate had emerged as the newest conspiracy about child sex trafficking. The conspiracy dealt with the idea that the furniture website Wayfair was a front for the selling of children. Social media users pointed to high-priced cabinets, pillows, and other furniture items as being named after missing children. Wayfair denied the claims and noted that some items were priced incorrectly and others were priced for industrial sales. Numerous independent fact-checks by journalists and organizations also stated that there was no truth to these claims, and even some of the supposed missing children came forward to say they were not missing. Despite this, in just over one week the hashtags #WayfairConspiracy and #WayfairGate grew larger and larger, amassing nearly 4.5 million views on TikTok (Seitz & Swenson, 2020).

The conspiracy grew so big, and so quickly, that the National Human Trafficking Hotline released a statement on July 20. The organization stated that they had received hundreds of calls about Wayfair in just a few days, none of which had been verified, and all of which were preventing the hotline from providing support to those in need (Polaris, 2020). Likewise, the National Center for Missing and Exploited Children and law enforcement agencies were also overwhelmed with false reports (Rajan et al., 2021). Local human trafficking organizations also spoke out in media interviews. For example, in a local media interview, the organization NC Stop Human Trafficking referred to Wayfairgate as a false narrative that obscures the reality of what child trafficking actually looks like (Kraft, 2020).

One analysis of Tweets within the first ten days of the hashtag appearing on Twitter found that Wayfairgate contained many of the classic elements of a moral panic (Hupp Williamson et al., 2023). Consensus was demonstrated with celebrities, influencers, and politicians sharing posts supporting the conspiracy (Greenspan, 2020; Seitz & Swenson, 2020). In fact, lifestyle and parenting influencers played a large role in helping to spread Wayfairgate on platforms such as Instagram (McNeal, 2020). False statistics were shared with real concern, and hostility directed at companies, celebrities, and politicians supposedly linked to Wayfairgate and the wider conspiracy of an international sex trafficking ring. Volatility of the panic was also seen. As quickly as the panic emerged and spread across social media platforms, it just as quickly moved from the general public's consciousness within a few months. One reason for people quickly moving on from Wayfairgate is perhaps due to a new hashtag that emerged the following month.

#SaveTheChildren emerged in conjunction with the UN-recognized World Day Against Trafficking in Persons on July 30, 2020. In the first week of August, the hashtag surged, and soon #SaveTheChildren received tens of millions of likes, shares, and comments on Facebook and Instagram. Several cities across the United States even became the location of in-person rallies to promote the movement (Funke, 2020). The broad message of this hashtag dealt with spreading generalized awareness about child sex trafficking, though sensationalized and extreme scenarios were still portrayed as typical (Rogers, 2020). Compared to previous conspiracies, the rallying cry of "Save the Children" acted "a kind of 'QAnon Lite' on-ramp—an issue QAnon believers could talk about openly without scaring off potential recruits with bizarre claims … and one that could pass nearly unnoticed in groups devoted to parenting, natural health and other nonpolitical topics" (Roose, 2020, para.10). This movement also saw high numbers of film and television celebrities as well as social media influencers using the hashtags (Moran & Prochaska, 2023). As one journalist pointed out, these posts can "drive the popularity of the hashtag, pulling in people—like younger women and those who aren't particularly politically engaged—who may be far outside QAnon's orbit" (North, 2020). With QAnon using the anti-trafficking movement to spread their talking points, misinformation about sex trafficking also spreads. This politicization of sex trafficking can also serve to create further divisions within the anti-trafficking movement and potentially lead to the misuse of resources.

General Rumors

More general rumors and fears of human trafficking also spread through social media. The anti-trafficking organization Polaris Project debunks several common ones on their website. This includes the rumor that traffickers mark vehicle windows of victims they aim to abduct with codes or zip-ties, the fear of white passenger or commercial vans which are used to transport trafficking victims, the use of abandoned child car seats to lure concerned women to help before kidnapping them, and that traffickers hand out drug-laced roses in order to obtain new sex trafficking victims (Polaris Project, 2020). In reality, none of these rumors have proven themselves to be founded and further distort the reality of how victims end up in trafficking situations.

Despite this, such rumors continue to pop up from time to time and rapidly spread through social media. Mom groups on Facebook and Instagram share tips on how to spot a trafficker and keep their children safe from abductors. As one illustration, consider the post from a New Jersey mom's Facebook group in 2020:

> just a quick heads up my daughter was in the beauty supply down by [H]ome [D]epot and in came a large gentleman with a mask that only showed his eyes and wearing a snowsuit. He proceeded to follow my daughter through the store [...], all the while motioning to a car a grey Toyota Camry type vehicle with tinted windows and a bad exhaust (note this is common with sex traffickers), that was waiting for him outside.
>
> (Benton & Peterka-Benton, 2021, p. 113)

Rumors like these emphasize extremes—abductions, schemes, and alarming numbers of missing children. In 2022, the National Center for Missing and Exploited Children (NCMEC) reported nearly 30,000 cases of missing children. The vast majority of missing children are runaways who may be counted more than once in the data if they run away more than once. Among the total cases of missing children recorded by the NCMEC, 4.5% of cases were family abductions (e.g., a parent who does not have custody), and 0.4% were nonfamily abductions (NCMEC, 2022). So, while abductions can occur in relation to child trafficking, research shows child victims are likely to be trafficked by someone they know, such as a friend, family member, or romantic partner (Lutnick, 2016).

Young women also perpetuate such stories on social media. For example, in 2021 a Target sex trafficking hoax went viral on TikTok. In dozens of videos, some of which garnered millions of views, young women described being followed by suspicious individuals in Target as an attempted trafficking operation (Dickson, 2021a). Experts describe such stories as urban legends, with the executive director of a national network of anti-trafficking advocates stating "I have never heard a case of anyone being abducted from Target in my 20 years in this field" (Dickson, 2021b, para.7). These rumors reach beyond social media as well when they are repeated by news media and politicians. In 2019 Baltimore Mayor Jack Young stated

> We're getting reports of somebody in a white van trying to snatch up young girls for human trafficking and for selling body parts, I'm told, so we have to really be careful, because there's so much evil going on, not just in the city of Baltimore, but around the country.
>
> (Herring, 2019, para.2)

He noted that this information was not coming from the local police, but Facebook.

Misinformation and Stereotypes

Perceptions of human trafficking are influenced by news media, popular culture, and social media. One study of residents in England found the three main sources of human trafficking information to be newspapers (77%), the internet (64%), and social media (50%) (Dando et al., 2016). With many individuals turning to social media as a source of information, it is not surprising to see increasing acceptance and endorsement of human trafficking myths and conspiracies. One survey of US college students found that 87.6% of all participants endorsed at least one human trafficking conspiracy, with the two most popular relating to women being at risk for sex trafficking while shopping and political elites running a global sex trafficking ring (Kenny et al., 2023). Stereotypes of human trafficking were also found, with participants conflating trafficking with smuggling, and believing that trafficking must involve both force and travel (Kenny et al., 2023).

Conspiracies that present distorted pictures of human trafficking have impacts beyond individuals' acceptance of myths. Survivors may not see themselves in these narratives and feel that police or social workers may not recognize them as trafficking victims (Dickson, 2021a). These conspiracies can also impact the ability of survivors to access services. Excessive reports of human trafficking to hotlines prevent actual victims and service providers from getting through and gaining access to resources. The operator of the US National Human Trafficking Hotline estimated that the time spent responding to false reports about Wayfairgate in the summer of 2020 was equivalent to working on responding to 42 actual trafficking cases (Rajan et al., 2021). A journalist for the *Washington Post* reported that human trafficking investigators at all 30 field offices of the Department of Homeland Security were forced to suspend ongoing investigations to respond to a flood of QAnon and Wayfair-inspired reports, resulting in delayed responses to genuine tips (Contrera, 2021).

The misinformation these conspiracies create is perpetuated by the "do it yourself" style of knowledge-seeking and sharing seen on social media (Goldenberg et al., 2021). Social media is viewed as a space where users can not only find information that is supposedly being hidden by mainstream media, but users can also share it themselves (Moran et al., 2023). Analysis of tweets during Wayfairgate emphasized this perspective, with users encouraging others to simply read through the associated hashtags to learn the "truth" (Hupp Williamson et al., 2023). Further, by simplifying the narrative into one that is good versus evil, anyone who tries to clarify misinformation can simply be dismissed as being on the "wrong moral side" (Moran et al., 2023).

As one scholar stated of human trafficking conspiracies: "rather than challenging the accounts of relevant powerful actors, they reinforce dominant narratives and institutions that shape anti-trafficking policies, and rather than democratizing knowledge, they undermine such efforts" (Watson, 2023, p. 1). Throughout all the above-examined conspiracies, an idealized picture of human trafficking is centered. Abducted women and girls are sold from the basement of a pizzeria or under the guise of a furniture retailer. Perpetrators are depicted as dangerous strangers, rather than individuals known to the victim who take advantage of aspects like poverty and mental health (Moran et al., 2023). Inaccurate and misleading statistics are repeated as evidence. Further, despite the widespread reach of QAnon globally, many of these conspiracies have focused exclusively on the trafficking of US citizens, ignoring the global picture of trafficking as well as migrant laborers' vulnerabilities (Watson, 2023).

In regard to policies, trafficking conspiracies also support measures that further control borders, movement, and sexuality (Watson, 2023). As one anti-trafficking program coordinator stated, "If you portray human trafficking as something that a secret cabal is doing, the solution becomes guns and surveillance. This is totally not the solution to trafficking" (Rogers, 2020, para.16). Human trafficking is reduced to forced prostitution, leaving uncriticized the root causes of trafficking. This means that root factors like homelessness, a chaotic home life, substance abuse issues, the child welfare system, and juvenile justice involvement are overlooked, despite their link to trafficking victimization (Feehs & Currier Wheeler, 2021; Twis, 2020).

The Role of the Internet

Throughout each of these conspiracies, the internet plays a central role—it is seen as a facilitator of trafficking in conspiracies like Wayfairgate and acts as a tool to spread and share such conspiracies. This next section explores the role of the internet, both as a tool in trafficking and as a focus of recent legislation.

As a Tool in Trafficking

The introduction of the internet and the growth of smartphones have been claimed to have dramatically contributed to an increase in human trafficking. This claim is frequently associated specifically with the sex trafficking of women and children with traffickers being depicted as bad individuals or organized crime groups (Milivojevic et al., 2020). In reality, there is a lack of knowledge about the extent that this technology facilitates trafficking, with existing research often based on small sample sizes. Sensationalized claims often get picked up and repeated by the media, law enforcement, and politicians. For example, one activist group claimed that underage sex trafficking on websites like Craigslist and Backpage rose exponentially in three US states. Their method for this assertion included asking a small group of people to guess the age of women in advertisements for sexual services. The guesses were then assumed to be correct, giving rise to the percentage of "underage" women on such websites (McNeill, 2021). Further, the relationship between technology and trafficking is often nuanced and complicated, as with many things regarding human trafficking.

In regard to recruitment, traffickers may use the internet to build online relationships with potential victims and post false or deceptive job advertisements. The internet can be used to facilitate trafficking through online postings for the sale of sexual services and used as a tool of control, with traffickers monitoring victims' online activity or threatening to "out" victims by sharing private information and photos. Data from three years of *potential* victims reported to the National Human Trafficking Hotline does indicate the use of internet-based recruiting, through websites such as Facebook, dating sites, Instagram, and more (Anthony, 2018). Among the 579 trafficking cases prosecuted in US federal courts in 2020, the internet was used to recruit victims in 41% of cases, with Facebook accounting for 59% of victim recruitment in sex trafficking cases (Feehs & Currier Wheeler, 2021). Facebook has also been shown to be a popular recruiting site in India, Nepal, Thailand, Hungary, and the United Kingdom (Sarkar, 2015). It is important to keep in mind, however, that these statistics may be skewed due to a bias toward prosecuting sex trafficking cases that involve an online element due to the investigative strategies often used by law enforcement. Studies show that police frequently monitor online advertisements for sexual services as a method to identify potential trafficking victims (Farrell et al., 2012; Nichols & Heil, 2015). In fact, it is estimated that 25 to 33% of sex trafficking cases are revealed through internet stings and search operations (Heil & Nichols, 2014).

Further, it is important to keep in mind that claiming an increase in trafficking due to technology may also be conflated with the fact that technology facilitates easier identification and tracking of trafficking cases. That is to say that technology and the internet are often also touted as a solution to trafficking. The internet and social media websites can be used to identify potential victims and to warn, assist, or rescue them (Milivojevic et al., 2020). This includes websites that inform victims of hotlines, assist with planning escape, and accessing resources post-trafficking. One survey found that 19% of survivors stated social media played a role in their exit from trafficking and 20% reported using private messages on social media to communicate with service providers (Anthony, 2018). Further, digital evidence can be helpful to criminal justice officials in building a case for prosecution, providing a way to move away from heavy reliance on victim testimony (Chen & Tortosa, 2020).

However, it is also important to be cautious of the many ways that technologically mediated surveillance is used in the name of protecting or rescuing victims, including the potential harms of such methods. For example, technology has been used to identify "suspicious" women at border entry points on the grounds that they may be sex workers. In Australia women who packed "sexy" clothes and underwear have been denied entry (Ham et al., 2013). Similarly, hotel chains such as the Marriott have been accused of training staff to "keep an eye" on women traveling alone in the name of anti-trafficking efforts (Brown, 2019). One anti-trafficking campaign from the US Department of Homeland Security encouraged hotel workers to look for people who appear tired, do not wish to have their rooms cleaned, have "sex paraphernalia," or a woman waiting to be picked up by a man (Brown, 2019). As with other anti-trafficking campaigns, these vague identifiers often lead to an over-policing of minorities, migrants, women, and sex workers.

Increasingly, automated or algorithmic techniques are being touted as technological innovations in the fight against human trafficking. This includes a wide variety of methods such as predictive analytics, facial recognition, data mining, mapping, computational linguistics, and the use of "big data" (Musto & Boyd, 2014). This often involves law enforcement partnering with third-party organizations who have such software. For example, actor Ashton Kutcher's anti-trafficking organization, renamed Thorn: Digital Defenders of Children, uses algorithmic software to scrape escort data in the hope of identifying sex trafficked children. Although the media claimed that this software "saved" over 6,000 children from sex trafficking, the truth was that the software had only identified potential cases of trafficking. In reality, 103 children were rescued (Mitchell, 2022). Further, consensual sex workers have complained that the software profiles them and shares their information with law enforcement, increasing their risk of harassment and arrest (Mitchell, 2022). The US DoD Defense Advanced Research Projects Administration developed a program called Memex that scraped data from the internet to build a database largely of adult advertisements with the intent of assisting human trafficking investigations. However, the $67 million spent on the software between 2014 and 2017 resulted in only three prosecutions (Brown, 2019). Further, as discussed in the previous chapter, there are many issues with attempting to use online advertisements for sexual services to make claims about sex trafficking. Researchers build their own assumptions into this technology, biasing the results. For example, in one study the use of cherry emojis in online advertisements was assumed to indicate virginity, though the researchers never stated how they came to that conclusion (Whitney et al., 2018).

Such algorithms frequently extend their surveillance beyond potential trafficking victims, to consensual sex workers. Airbnb, DoorDash, and PayPal all have a history of banning users suspected of being sex workers and even those associated with potential sex workers such as friends and partners (Snow, 2022). Airbnb uses AI technology to rate users "trustworthiness." A journalist reports that the patent for this technology cites traits such as involvement in sex work or pornography, drug use and criminal records, and personality and mental health traits such as "badness" and "neuroticism" (Snow, 2022).

Ultimately, when media, politicians, and even academics focus on technology as a primary force behind human trafficking, governments then have little incentive to address the root causes tied to vulnerability and exploitation. The perspective becomes that technology and online spaces must be securitized in order to protect women and children from traffickers, leading to surveillance of everyone. The problem lies in that there is no easy way to distinguish those who use technology as responsible citizens from criminals and therefore no realistic way to entirely remove sexual content from the internet (Mendel & Sharapov, 2016).

As a Focus of Legislation

Many of the arguments about the internet's relationship with trafficking have centered not on social media websites, such as Facebook or Instagram, but on online classified ad websites like Craigslist and Backpage. Beginning around 2008, both child welfare and anti-trafficking groups focused their attention on these websites, arguing that they facilitate trafficking through advertisements for sexual services (Musto, 2016). A report from the US Government Accountability Office notes that

> In 2010, craigslist.org was the leading platform in the online commercial sex market. However, under pressure from 17 state attorneys general who were concerned about the use of craigslist.org for purposes of prostitution and sex trafficking, craigslist.org voluntarily removed its "adult" section in September 2010. Afterward, buyers and sellers shifted toward using backpage.com, which then emerged as the market leader.
>
> (GAO, 2021, p. 10)

The next significant event would occur in June 2014, when the FBI seized myredbook.com and later convicted the website operator for facilitating prostitution (GAO, 2021). Since 1999, MyRedBook had hosted ads for escorts and massage services in addition to a chatroom for largely female sex workers and male clients to exchange information about services and safety (Majic, 2020). The raid and closure of a similar website for male escorts, rentboy.com, occurred in 2015, though media did not connect this site with human trafficking in the same way as sites hosting female ads. In fact, responses to the closure of RentBoy highlighted gay men's sexual freedom and called for the decriminalization of prostitution, something that had not occurred with the closure of MyRedBook (Majic, 2020). Then, in April 2018, federal authorities seized backpage.com and only five days later the largest piece of federal legislation dealing with the relationship between sex trafficking and the internet would be enacted (GAO, 2021).

FOSTA (Allow States and Victims to Fight Online Sex Trafficking Act) and SESTA (Stop Enabling Sex Traffickers Act) were bills that emerged from the US Senate and House. In the legislative debate for these bills, legislators made claims about the prevalence of sex trafficking on such sites without data or evidence to support their claims (Gezinski & Gonzalez-Pons, 2022). Rhetoric also reflected stereotypes about human trafficking victims and offenders, with an emphasis on women and children being sexually exploited by men (Eichert, 2019). When FOSTA-SESTA was enacted in 2018, the stated goal was to "reduce human trafficking by amending Section 230 of the Communications Decency Act and holding Internet platforms accountable for the content their users post" (Blunt & Wolf, 2020, p. 117). Previously, web publishers were protected as the law distinguished between content that users post and content that web providers themselves distribute (Gezinski & Gonzalez-Pons, 2022). The resulting effect was that many web platforms, including Facebook, Tumblr, and Reddit, revised their guidelines or simply removed adult content to avoid even the possibility of legal liability (Born, 2019). The law has not greatly increased human trafficking prosecutions, as between 2018 and 2021, only one federal prosecution occurred under the new law (Mathias, 2023). Conversely, evidence suggests that the usefulness of the law in regard to legal accountability is outweighed by the negative impacts of the law on both consensual sex workers and law enforcement's ability to identify victims and offenders.

Laws like FOSTA–SESTA overlook the usefulness that classified ad websites provide in the investigation of trafficking cases. This includes using such websites to conduct stings and other undercover operations or using site data and evidence to build cases for successful prosecution. Historically, such platforms actively worked with law enforcement through trainings that provided information on how to use their data in trafficking investigations or responded to subpoena requests (Musto, 2016). When such websites are forced to close because of legislation like FOSTA–SESTA, online trafficking activities are not eliminated. They simply move, and they move to websites that may be on the dark web or hosted in other countries that have no responsibility to respond to a subpoena. Traffickers that do continue to advertise victims on such websites simply become more creative with their postings or move ads to harder-to-trace websites, only working to make victims harder to locate (Heil & Nichols, 2014). A 2019 FBI document admitted that the ability of law enforcement to identify and locate both trafficking victims and offenders significantly decreased following the closure of backpage.com (GAO, 2021).

Such legislation also collapses consensual sex work with sex trafficking and ignores the usefulness of such websites for sex workers. One survey of sex workers about the effects of FOSTA–SESTA found that sex workers lost the ability to work independently and were forced to return to more exploitative working conditions on the street or involving third parties. Digital safety precautions such as screening clients, online payment, and lists of clients to avoid were also lost (Blunt & Wolf, 2020). With websites often working across geographical boundaries, the effects reached beyond the United States as well, with sex workers in Australia, France, and New Zealand reporting similar concerns after FOSTA–SESTA passage (Musto et al., 2021).

Such legislation also has the potential to widen beyond the domain of human trafficking, to include various forms of sex work, such as prostitution, pornography, commercial stripping, erotic webcam performances, and even sugar-dating websites (Weitzer, 2020). While prostitution has long been conflated with sex trafficking, the introduction of the internet has allowed for pornography to begin to be included as well, often without credible evidence. Critics argue that pornography breaks apart families and normalizes violence toward women and children, though this concern is often disproportionate to actual harm (Weitzer, 2020). In 2023, several US states began passing laws requiring users to verify their ages to visit adult websites. In response, notable websites such as Pornhub have removed their web access in such states. The Free Speech Coalition's director of public affairs noted: "it's important to understand that these laws are less about protecting minors, and more about restricting the open Internet. State-level regulations that primarily target adult sites are tremendously ineffective at keeping minors from accessing adult content" (Belanger, 2023, para.6). This is because the vagueness of the laws means that they impact more than adult websites, with a written "description of a female nipple" being enough to induce liability in some states.

As moral panics around sex and human trafficking continue to persist, they should be critically examined in regard to their ability to impact public opinion, guide anti-trafficking resource distribution, and even shape policy. Boettcher (2022, p. 217) notes:

> In the wake of QAnon's viral proliferation, there was a spike in bills-which almost universally had bipartisan co-sponsorship and many of which were introduced by Democrats-which would have expanded criminal penalties or increased funding to prosecution or law enforcement efforts to combat the very boogeymen that QAnon and mainstream trafficking organizations point toward.

Moving forward, researchers and policymakers must critically study the relationship between technology, social media, and human trafficking, including the unintended impacts of legislation on aspects such as investigation and the safety of consensual sex workers.

7 Conclusion

The history of human trafficking is one that is intertwined with moral panics. From the early panics about a slave trade in White women in the nineteenth century, to more modern panics around sporting events and social media, the topic of human trafficking has never strayed far from oversimplified yet sensationalized depictions. Through the lens of cultural criminology, this book set out to unravel this history and explore the relationship between human trafficking, moral panics, and media coverage. Chapter 3 explored the origins of human trafficking panics with the White slave panic at the turn of the nineteenth century and its re-emergence at the end of the twentieth century. The chapter contrasted the moral entrepreneurs and media coverage in each period while highlighting the impact of the panic on laws. Chapter 4 explored the role of pop culture in creating human trafficking panics, through television and films, awareness raising, and celebrity campaigns. Pop culture panics were shown to shape public beliefs and reinforce stereotypes about human trafficking. Chapter 5 turned to sporting event panics, with mega-sporting events such as the Olympics, World Cup, and Super Bowl claiming to be hot spots for human trafficking. The evidence for these claims was highly dubious, with such panics instead negatively impacting sex workers who are not trafficking victims. Finally, Chapter 6 looked at the ways that modern technology, and specifically social media, shapes human trafficking panics. This included the use of hashtags and online social movements in generating misinformation as well as the role that internet plays in human trafficking and how legislation is trying to tackle the issue.

Throughout each of these chapters, the pieces of moral panic are seen time and time again. As discussed in Chapter 2, there are many theories on what causes moral panics, including changes in the social, economic, or moral order of society. In the context of the White slave panic, the early nineteenth century was fraught with many societal changes. Developments in transportation technology facilitated large increases in migration between the late 1800s and early 1900s. There were changes to the family structure, and the independence of women grew as many women migrated. It is against this backdrop that one of the first human trafficking panics can be understood. Many of

DOI: 10.4324/9781003439004-7

the myths around White slavery were grounded in concerns about women's sexuality and foreigners' threat to national identity. Campaigns against White slavery focused on White women as victims of foreign men and emphasized the sexual dangers of venturing outside the safety of marriage and family.

The re-emergence of panic around the sex trafficking of women in the 1990s and 2000s reflected ~~many~~ similar themes around social anxiety and change. While immigration declined greatly following World War I, starting in 1989 there was an 11-year period of heightened migration into the United States. Further, the feminization of international migration also grew, with female migrants now accounting for nearly half of all migrants. While the White slave panic focused on European women forced into prostitution in the Americas, today the focus is on women trafficked to Western Europe and the United States from Latin America, Asia, and the former Soviet Union. The threat of migrants, and particularly those working as prostitutes, has persisted and is often connected with organized crime and terrorism.

Much of the rhetoric around migration and trafficking between the two periods is similar. During the White slave panic, anxieties about women's movement and increasing independence were reflected in posters that warned girls about going abroad or into the city. Today, anti-trafficking campaigns reflect similar themes and warn about the "sexual dangers of life away from home and hearth" (Doezema, 2010, p. 126). As with the White slave panic of the early twentieth century, many modern campaigns also discourage migration and specifically women's migration. Women's migration is often portrayed as dangerous, leading to forced prostitution, and so the safe solution is to simply remain at home.

Beyond these societal shifts, other favorable conditions can also be identified as generating a moral panic. These include the ability of the media to draw rival claims from various agencies and interest groups, a narrative that is accessible to the general public with identifiable heroes and villains, and visual elements that can perpetuate stereotypes about the issue (Jenkins, 2009). Human trafficking panics reflect many of these elements. Regarding rival interest groups, there is a longstanding tension between those that view prostitution and consensual sex work as distinct from human trafficking and those that do not. The moral entrepreneurs involved in modern human trafficking narratives include a broad variety of groups and organizations, with some reaching greater influence than others. This includes feminist groups, religious groups, and human rights organizations. Feminists remain split on the issue of prostitution, with some groups arguing that there is no such thing as voluntary prostitution, while other groups distinguish between voluntary and forced prostitution. The former viewpoint is represented by the Coalition Against Trafficking in Women (CATW) while the latter is represented by the Global Alliance Against Traffic in Women (GAATW), two highly influential anti-trafficking groups. The abolitionist feminist groups have often worked alongside organizations of the religious right, believe prostitution and sex trafficking to be inextricably linked, deny the possibility of agency and consent within sex work, and believe the legalization of sex work would worsen the situation.

The narratives that are presented to the public through ~~the~~ media also reflect simplified and sensationalized versions of human trafficking, with tropes about victims, villains, and rescuers. Media representations of human trafficking have consistently stereotyped what both victims and villains look like, contributing to the idea of the "ideal victim" and "ideal offender." The ideal trafficking victim is a victim of sex trafficking, female, and young. She also lacks agency, with victims not choosing to participate in sex work, and therefore is helpless and blameless. A typical trafficking narrative may sensationalize the violence experienced by a girl lured to the West by the promise of a job or marriage, her innocence emphasized through her youth and virginity. Traffickers are stereotyped as male foreigners with no relationship to their victims who use physical force to control them, while rescuers are frequently portrayed as American in contrast to foreign traffickers. These stereotypes are perpetuated in visual representations of trafficking, in fictional films like *Taken* and *Trade*, in documentary portrayals, and even in awareness campaigns. This media often presents a narrow view of human trafficking, focusing on young female victims who are abducted or deceived into forced prostitution. Villains are, portrayed as part of organized crime gangs. These sensationalized depictions of human trafficking divert resources from labor trafficking and lead to an under-identification of legitimate victims. Migrants and sex workers experiencing exploitation often face criminalization rather than receive help. Further, the media's framing of the issue of human trafficking as primarily a crime and justice problem obscures the structural factors that leave individuals vulnerable to trafficking in the first place. By using a simplified victim and villain narrative, human trafficking is reduced to an individual problem remedied by law enforcement and charity. This isolation overlooks the complex role that factors like poverty, discrimination, and demand for cheap labor all play.

Reactions are also a crucial element of moral panics. These reactions may come from mass media, the press, the public, agencies of social control, lawmakers and politicians, or action groups. Each chapter throughout this book has explored the consequences of, or the reactions to, these human trafficking panics. This includes influencing legislation that was passed, from the Mann Act in 1910 to the Trafficking Victims Protection Act in 2000. Under the TVPA, trafficking into commercial sex is symbolically privileged over other forms of trafficking. A well-studied outcome of this separation under the law is how human trafficking is often reduced to sex trafficking, with training and resources prioritizing sex trafficking, and labor trafficking treated only as an afterthought. Further, sex trafficking cases are identified, investigated, and prosecuted at a higher rate compared to labor trafficking cases. More recent panics about social media and websites' role in sex trafficking have led to hasty new laws, such as FOSTA-SESTA in 2018. The law has not greatly increased human trafficking prosecutions, as between 2018 and 2021, only one federal prosecution has occurred under the new law. Conversely, evidence suggests that the usefulness of the law with regard to legal accountability is outweighed by the negative impacts of the law on both consensual sex workers and law enforcement's ability to identify victims and offenders.

Frequently, a moral panic leads to a stage where law enforcement and politicians "crack down" and "get tough" on the activity related to the panic. Countries restrict women's migration, and police and deport sex workers, all in the name of anti-trafficking work. This is seen in the reactions to the panic about trafficking around mega-sporting events, which have disproportionately emphasized sex trafficking. In the run-up to such events, police have employed the use of raids to identify and "rescue" trafficking victims. Yet such raids have not proven to be a highly successful method of identifying trafficking victims. Instead, they are likely to increase sex workers' vulnerability and exposure to violence as their work is driven further underground, while also creating a climate of fear and distrust with the authorities.

Drawing from Goode and Ben-Yehuda (1994), the five elements of a moral panic are also threaded throughout this book. Heightened concern and widespread consensus are seen in the growth of academic articles and journals dealing with human trafficking, news investigations and films about the topic, newly proposed laws, and increasing numbers of groups, including both formal anti-trafficking organizations and social media groups centered around the issue. The hostility element is aimed at the group deemed responsible for the threatening behavior and often relies on stereotyping. Regarding human trafficking, hostility has been directed at various groups, including sex workers and immigrants. Disproportionality occurs when facts and statistics about the reality of the problem are non-existent or greatly exaggerated. This is certainly present in human trafficking panics, as seen with sporting event panics. Unverifiable claims have been repeated by prostitution abolitionist groups, politicians, and journalists, with estimated figures of victims ranging from 10,000 to 100,000 at each sporting event. Finally, volatility is seen in the way that these panics seem to ebb and flow over time. The White slave panic of the early nineteenth century died out, only to reemerge at the end of the twentieth century. Sporting event panics are not continuous, but emerge every four years around events such as the World Cup and Olympics. Social media panics are perhaps the most volatile, with hashtags such as Wayfairgate remaining popular for only weeks at a time.

As moral panics around human trafficking continue to persist, they should continue to be critically examined with regard to their ability to impact public opinion, guide anti-trafficking resource distribution, and even shape policy. These moral panics persevere for many reasons: they are useful strategies for fundraising, provide stories that grab the media and public's attention, and justify various social control measures aimed at migrants and sex workers

(Ham, 2011). As this book has shown though, many of the anti-trafficking efforts that emerge from these panics are uncritical or misinformed, resulting in human rights violations against vulnerable groups (GAATW, 2007). Sex work and human trafficking are conflated, with women locked up in detention shelters in the name of rescue, or deported back to their original situation of vulnerability. Labor trafficking and the exploitation of men is overlooked and underfunded. To truly tackle the issue of trafficking, media and policy-makers must acknowledge the root factors of vulnerability to trafficking and the specific needs of victims must be addressed, all while working to protect migrants, sex workers, and the agency of victims.

References

Agustín, L. M. (2005). Migrants in the mistress's house: Other voices in the "trafficking" debate. *Social Politics: International Studies in Gender, State and Society*, *12*(1), 96–117.

Ahmed, A., & Seshu, M. (2012). "We have the right not to be 'rescued'..."*: When anti- trafficking programmes undermine the health and well-being of sex workers. *Anti- Trafficking Review*, *1*, 149–161.

Akee, R. K. Q., Basu, A. K., Chau, N. H., & Khamis, M. (2010). Ethnic fragmentation, conflict, displaced persons and human trafficking: An empirical analysis. In G. S. Epstein & I. N. Gang (Eds.), *Migration and culture: Frontiers of economics and globalization* (Vol. 8, pp. 691–716). Emerald Group Publishing.

Al Thani, M. (2021). Channelling soft power: The Qatar 2022 World Cup, Migrant Workers, and international image. *The International Journal of the History of Sport*, *38*(17), 1729–1752.

Albright, E., & D'Adamo, K. (2017). Decreasing human trafficking through sex work decriminalization. *AMA journal of ethics*, *19*(1), 122-126.

Altheide, D. L. (2009). Moral panic: From sociological concept to public discourse. *Crime, Media, Culture*, *5*(1), 79–99.

Anderson, K. L. (2015). *Cases of forced labor and policy responses regarding human trafficking legislation at mega sporting events* [Thesis, University of Kansas].

Andrijasevic, R. (2007). Beautiful dead bodies: Gender, migration and representation in anti- trafficking campaigns. *Feminist Review*, *86*(1), 24–44.

Anthony, B. (2018). *On-ramps, intersections, and exit routes: A roadmap for systems and industries to prevent and disrupt human trafficking*. Polaris Project. https://polarisproject.org/wp-content/uploads/2018/08/A-Roadmap-for-Systems-and-Industries-to-Prevent-and-Disrupt-Human-Trafficking-Social-Media.pdf

Aronowitz, A. A. (2009). The smuggling – trafficking nexus and the myths surrounding human trafficking. In W. F. Mcdonald (Ed.), *Immigration, crime and justice* (Vol. 13, pp. 107–128). Emerald Group Publishing Limited.

Aronowitz, A. A. (2017). *Human trafficking: A reference handbook*. ABC-CLIO.

Arthurs, J. (2012). Distant suffering, proper distance: Cosmopolitan ethics in the film portrayal of trafficked women. *International Journal of Media & Cultural Politics*, *8*(2–3), 141–158.

Attwood, R. (2015). Stopping the traffic: The national vigilance association and the international fight against the 'white slave' trade (1899–c.1909). *Women's History Review*, *24*(3), 325–350.

Attwood, R. (2016). Looking beyond 'White Slavery': Trafficking, the Jewish Association, and the dangerous politics of migration control in England, 1890–1910. *Anti-Trafficking Review*, *7*, 1–10.

Austin, R. (2016). *Human trafficking in the media: A content analysis on human trafficking frames in documentaries, movies, and television episodes* [M.S., Northeastern University].

Austin, R., & Farrell, A. (2017, April 26). *Human trafficking and the media in the United States*. Oxford Research Encyclopedia of Criminology and Criminal Justice.

Avdeyeva, O. A. (2012). Does reputation matter for states' compliance with international treaties? States enforcement of anti-trafficking norms. *The International Journal of Human Rights*, *16*(2), 298–320.

Baker, C. N. (2014). An intersectional analysis of sex trafficking films. *Meridians*, *12*(1), 208–226.

Bales, K. (2004). *Disposable people: New slavery in the global economy* (2nd ed.). University of California Press.

Bales, K. (2005). The challenge of measuring slavery. In K. Bales (Ed.), *Understanding global slavery: A reader* (pp. 87–111). University of California Press.

Bales, K., Murphy, L. T., & Silverman, B. W. (2020). How many trafficked people are there in Greater New Orleans? Lessons in measurement. *Journal of Human Trafficking*, *6*(4), 375–387.

Balgamwalla, S. (2016). Trafficking in narratives: Conceptualizing and recasting victims, offenders, and rescuers in the war on human trafficking. *Denver Law Review*, *94*(1), 1–42.

Barak, G. (1988). Newsmaking criminology: Reflections on the media, intellectuals, and crime articles on critical criminology. *Justice Quarterly*, *5*(4), 565–588.

Barak, G. (1995). Media, society, and criminology. In G. Barak (Ed.), *Media, process, and the social construction of crime* (pp. 3–46). Routledge.

Barnhart, M. H. (2009). Sex and slavery: An analysis of three models of state human trafficking legislation. *William & Mary Journal of Women and the Law*, *16*(1), 83–132.

Barrick, K., Lattimore, P. K., Pitts, W. J., & Zhang, S. X. (2014). When farmworkers and advocates see trafficking but law enforcement does not: Challenges in identifying labor trafficking in North Carolina. *Crime, Law and Social Change*, *61*(2), 205–214.

Becker, H. S. (1963). *Outsiders: Studies in the sociology of deviance*. The Free Press.

Beckman, M. D. (1983). The White slave traffic act: The historical impact of a criminal law policy on women notes. *Georgetown Law Journal*, *72*(3), 1111–1142.

Belanger, A. (2023, July 3). *Pornhub cuts off more US users in ongoing protest over age- verification laws*. Ars Technica. https://arstechnica.com/tech-policy/2023/07/free-speech-group-backs-pornhub-in-fight-against-state-age-verification-laws/

Benton, B., & Peterka-Benton, D. (2012). When the abyss looks back: Treatments of human trafficking in superhero comic books. *The Popular Culture Studies Journal*. https://digitalcommons.montclair.edu/justice-studies-facpubs/184

Benton, B., & Peterka-Benton, D. (2021). Truth as a victim: The challenge of anti-trafficking education in the age of Q. *Anti-Trafficking Review*, *17*, 113–131.

Ben-Yehuda, N. (2009). Foreword: Moral panics—36 years on. *The British Journal of Criminology*, *49*(1), 1–3.

Berger, P. L., & Luckmann, T. (1967). *The social construction of reality: A treatise in the sociology of knowledge*. Knopf Doubleday Publishing Group.

Bernburg, J. (2019). Labeling theory. In M. D. Krohn, N. Hendrix, G. P. Hall, & A. J. Lizotte (Eds.), *Handbook of crime and deviance* (2nd ed., pp. 179–196).

Bernstein, E. (2007). The sexual politics of the "new abolitionism." *Differences: A Journal of Feminist Cultural Studies*, *18*(3), 128–151.

Best, J. (2013). *Social problems*. W.W. Norton & Company.

Beyer, C. (2018). "In the suitcase was a boy": Representing transnational child trafficking in contemporary crime fiction. In C. Gregoriou (Ed.), *Representations of transnational human trafficking: Present-day news media, true crime, and fiction* (pp. 89–116). Springer International Publishing.

Birks, J., & Gardner, A. (2019). Introducing the slave next door. *Anti-Trafficking Review*, *13*, 66–81.

Blakemore, E. (2017, October 11). Jane Addams's Crusade against Victorian "Dancing Girls." *JSTOR Daily*. https://daily.jstor.org/jane-addams-crusade-victorian-dancing-girls/

Blunt, D., & Wolf, A. (2020). Erased: The impact of FOSTA-SESTA and the removal of backpage on sex workers. *Anti-Trafficking Review*, *14*, 117–121.

Boecking, B., Miller, K., Kennedy, E., & Dubrawski, A. (2019). Quantifying the relationship between large public events and escort advertising behavior. *Journal of Human Trafficking*, *5*(3), 220–237.

Boettcher, A. S. (2022). QAnon: What the viral conspiracy theory can teach us about the mainstream sex trafficking debate. *Berkeley Journal of Gender, Law & Justice*, *37*, 195–220.

Boff, A. (2012). *Silence on violence: Improving safety of women*. London Assembly Member. glaconservatives.co.uk/silence-on-violence/

Bohm, R. M., & Vogel, B. L. (2015). *A primer on crime and delinquency theory* (4th ed.). Carolina Academic Press.

Boggiani, M. (2015). When Is a Trafficking Victim a Trafficking Victim: Anti-Prostitution Statutes and Victim Protection. *Cleveland State Law Review*, 64, 915-964.

Bonthuys, E. (2012). The 2010 Football World Cup and the regulation of sex work in South Africa. *Journal of Southern African Studies*, *38*(1), 11–29.

Boris, E., & Berg, H. (2014). Protecting virtue, erasing labor: Historical responses to trafficking. In K. K. Hoang & R. S. Parrenas (Eds.), *Human trafficking reconsidered: Rethinking the problem, envisioning new solutions* (pp. 19–40). The International Debate Education Association.

Born, E. J. (2019). Too far and not far enough: Understanding the impact of FOSTA. *NYU Law Review*, *94*, 1623–1653.

Bouché, V., Farrell, A., & Wittmer, D. (2015). *Identifying effective counter-trafficking programs and practices in the U.S.: Legislative, legal, and public opinion strategies that work* (p. 95). US Department of Justice. https://www.ojp.gov/pdffiles1/nij/grants/249670.pdf

Bouché, V., Farrell, A., & Wittmer-Wolfe, D. E. (2018). Challenging the dominant frame: The moderating impact of exposure and knowledge on perceptions of sex trafficking victimization*. *Social Science Quarterly*, *99*(4), 1283–1302.

Boukli, A., & Renz, F. (2019). Deconstructing the lesbian, gay, bisexual, transgender victim of sex trafficking: Harm, exceptionality and religion–sexuality tensions. *International Review of Victimology*, 25(1), 71-90.

Bowen and Shannon Frontline Consulting. (2009). *Human trafficking, sex work safety and the 2010 games*. Sex Industry Worker Safety Action Group. https://www.nswp

.org/resource/member-publications/human-trafficking-sex-work-safety-and-the-2010-games

Bowersox, Z. (2016). International sporting events and human trafficking: Effects of mega- events on a state's capacity to address human trafficking. *Journal of Human Trafficking*, *2*(3), 201–220.

Bradley, C., & Szablewska, N. (2016). Anti-trafficking (ILL-)efforts: The legal regulation of women's bodies and relationships in Cambodia. *Social & Legal Studies; London*, *25*(4), 461.

Brown, E. N. (2019, February 5). Are you a woman traveling alone? Marriott might be watching you. *Reason.Com*. https://reason.com/2019/02/05/hotel-surveillance-state-sex-trafficking/

Bryant-Davis, T., & Tummala-Narra, P. (2017). Cultural oppression and human trafficking: Exploring the role of racism and ethnic bias. *Women & Therapy*, *40*(1–2), 152–169.

Buchanan, J. (2013). *Race to the bottom: Exploitation of migrant workers ahead of Russia's 2014 Winter Olympic Games in Sochi*. Human Rights Watch. https://www.hrw.org/report/2013/02/06/race-bottom/exploitation-migrant-workers-ahead-russias-2014-winter-olympic-games

Buckley, M. (2009). Public opinion in Russia on the politics of human trafficking. *Europe- Asia Studies*, *61*(2), 213–248.

Buntain, C., Barlow, M. D., Bloom, M., & Johns, M. A. (2022). Paved with bad intentions: QAnon's save the children campaign. *Journal of Online Trust and Safety*, *1*(2), 1–28.

Busza, J., Castle, S., & Diarra, A. (2004). Trafficking and health. *BMJ : British Medical Journal*, *328*(7452), 1369–1371.

Butler, C. N. (2015). The racial roots of human trafficking. *UCLA Law Review*, *62*(6), 1464–1514.

Byford, J. (2011). *Conspiracy theories: A critical introduction*. Palgrave Macmillan.

Cameron, S., & Newman, E. (2008). Introduction: Understanding human trafficking. In S. Cameron & E. Newman (Eds.), *Trafficking in humans: Social, cultural and political dimensions* (pp. 1–18). United Nations University Press.

Casassa, K., Knight, L., & Mengo, C. (2022). Trauma bonding perspectives from service providers and survivors of sex trafficking: A scoping review. *Trauma, Violence, & Abuse*, *23*(3), 969–984.

Chacón, J. M. (2006). Misery and Myopia: Understanding the failures of U.S. efforts to stop human trafficking part IV: Asylum, refugees, and human rights. *Immigration and Nationality Law Review*, *27*, 331–396.

Chambers, R., Gibson, M., Chaffin, S., Takagi, T., Nguyen, N., & Mears-Clark, T. (2024). Trauma-coerced attachment and complex PTSD: Informed care for survivors of human trafficking. *Journal of Human Trafficking*, *10*(1), 41–50.

Chapkis, W. (2003). Trafficking, migration, and the law: Protecting innocents, punishing immigrants. *Gender & Society*, *17*(6), 923–937.

Chen, I., & Tortosa, C. (2020). The use of digital evidence in human trafficking investigations. *Anti-Trafficking Review*, *14*, Article 122–124.

Cho, S.-Y., Dreher, A., & Neumayer, E. (2014). Determinants of anti-trafficking policies: Evidence from a new index. *The Scandinavian Journal of Economics*, *116*(2), 429–454.

Cho, S.-Y., & Vadlamannati, K. C. (2012). Compliance with the anti-trafficking protocol. *European Journal of Political Economy*, *28*(2), 249–265.

Chong, N. G. (2014). Human trafficking and sex industry: Does ethnicity and race matter? *Journal of Intercultural Studies*, *35*(2), 196–213.

Chow, C. (2020). Decolonizing human trafficking in cambodia special coverage: Global. *Human Rights Brief*, *23*, 59–61.

Christenson, H. (2018). For the game. For the world. But what about for the workers? Evaluating FIFA's Human Rights Policy in relation to international standards comments. *San Diego International Law Journal*, *20*, 93–126.

Christie, N. (1986). The Ideal Victim. In *From Crime Policy to Victim Policy: Reorienting the Justice System*, edited by Ezzat A. Fattah, 17–30. London: Palgrave Macmillan UK.

Chuang, J. (2006). Beyond a snapshot: Preventing human trafficking in the global economy. *Indiana Journal of Global Legal Studies*, *13*(1), 137–163.

Chuang, J. A. (2010). Rescuing trafficking from ideological capture: Prostitution reform and anti-trafficking law and policy. *University of Pennsylvania Law Review*, *158*(6), 1655–1728.

Chuang, J. A. (2014). Exploitation creep and the unmaking of human trafficking law. *The American Journal of International Law*, *108*(4), 609–649.

Cockbain, E., & Bowers, K. (2019). Human trafficking for sex, labour and domestic servitude: How do key trafficking types compare and what are their predictors? *Crime, Law and Social Change*, *72*(1), 9–34.

Cockbain, E., Bowers, K., & Dimitrova, G. (2018). Human trafficking for labour exploitation: The results of a two-phase systematic review mapping the European evidence base and synthesising key scientific research evidence. *Journal of Experimental Criminology*, *14*(3), 319–360.

Cohen, S. (1972). *Folk devils and moral panics: The creation of the mods and rockers*. Routledge.

Cohen, S. (2011). Whose side were we on? The undeclared politics of moral panic theory. *Crime, Media, Culture*, *7*(3), 237–243.

Cojocaru, C. (2015). Sex trafficking, captivity, and narrative: Constructing victimhood with the goal of salvation. *Dialectical Anthropology*, *39*(2), 183–194.

Conklin, M., Cizmar, K., & Hinman, E. E. (2011, June 29). Real men get their facts straight. *The Village Voice*. https://www.villagevoice.com/real-men-get-their-facts-straight/

Contrera, J. (2021, December 16). A QAnon con: How the viral Wayfair sex trafficking lie hurt real kids. *Washington Post*. https://www.washingtonpost.com/dc-md-va/interactive/2021/wayfair-qanon-sex-trafficking-conspiracy/

Convention for the Suppression of the Traffic in Persons and of the Exploitation of the Prostitution of Others, December 2, 1949, https://www.ohchr.org/en/instruments-mechanisms/instruments/convention-suppression-traffic-persons-and-exploitation

Corrin, C. (2005). Transitional road for traffic: Analysing trafficking in women from and through Central and Eastern Europe. *Europe-Asia Studies*, *57*(4), 543–560.

Cree, V. E., Clapton, G., & Smith, M. (2014). The presentation of child trafficking in the UK: An old and new moral panic? *The British Journal of Social Work*, *44*(2), 418–433.

Critcher, C. (2008). Moral panic analysis: Past, present and future. *Sociology Compass*, *2*(4), 1127–1144.

Critcher, C. (2011). For a political economy of moral panics. *Crime, Media, Culture*, *7*(3), 259–275.

CTDC. (2021). *Counter-Trafficking Data Collaborative*. Counter-Trafficking Data Collaborative. https://www.ctdatacollaborative.org/

Cunha, A., Gonçalves, M., & Matos, M. (2022). Exploring perceptions of Portuguese police about human trafficking victims and perpetrators. *Crime, Law and Social Change*, *77*(3), 253–273.

Cunningham, K. C., & Cromer, L. D. (2016). Attitudes about human trafficking: Individual differences related to belief and victim blame. *Journal of Interpersonal Violence*, *31*(2), 228–244.

Dando, C. J., Walsh, D., & Brierley, R. (2016). Perceptions of psychological coercion and human trafficking in the West Midlands of England: Beginning to know the unknown. *PLoS One*, *11*(5), e0153263.

David, M., Rohloff, A., Petley, J., & Hughes, J. (2011). The idea of moral panic – ten dimensions of dispute. *Crime, Media, Culture*, *7*(3), 215–228.

Davidson, J. O. (2017). Editorial: The presence of the past: Lessons of history for anti-trafficking work. *Anti-Trafficking Review*, *9*, 1–12.

De Shalit, A. (2014). Human trafficking and media myths: Federal funding, communication strategies, and Canadian anti-trafficking programs. *Canadian Journal of Communication*, *39*(3), 385–412.

de Villiers, N. (2016). Rebooting trafficking. *Anti-Trafficking Review*, *7*, Article 7.

de Vries, I., Nickerson, C., Farrell, A., Wittmer-Wolfe, D. E., & Bouché, V. (2019). Anti- immigration sentiment and public opinion on human trafficking. *Crime, Law and Social Change*, *72*(1), 125–143.

De Vries, P. (2005). White slaves in a colonial nation: The Dutch campaign against the traffic in women in the early twentieth century. *Social & Legal Studies*, *14*(1), 39–60.

Deering, K. N., Chettiar, J., Chan, K., Taylor, M., Montaner, J. S., & Shannon, K. (2012). Sex work and the public health impacts of the 2010 Olympic Games. *Sexually Transmitted Infections*, *88*(4), 301–303.

Deering, K., & Shannon, K. (2012). Fears of an influx of sex workers to major sporting events are unfounded. *BMJ*, *345*, e5845.

DeKeseredy, W. S., & Dragiewicz, M. (2011). *Handbook of critical criminology*. Routledge.

Delva, W., Richter, M., Koker, P. D., Chersich, M., & Temmerman, M. (2011). Sex Work during the 2010 FIFA World Cup: Results from a three-wave cross-sectional survey. *PLoS One*, *6*(12), e28363.

Derks, A., Henke, R., & Vanna, L. (2006). *Review of a decade of research on trafficking in persons, Cambodia*. The Asia Foundation. https://asiafoundation.org/resources/pdfs/CBTIPreview.pdf

Dickson, E. (2021a, April 7). Target sex-trafficking Hoax going viral on TikTok. *Rolling Stone*. https://www.rollingstone.com/culture/culture-features/target-sex-trafficking-tiktok-hoax-1151665/

Dickson, E. (2021b, July 15). A video spreading conspiracy theories about a satanic sex- trafficking ring is going viral. *Rolling Stone*. https://www.rollingstone.com/culture/culture-features/sex-trafficking-qanon-documentary-tiktok-1197269/

Dickson, E. (2023). 'Sound of freedom' torched by child-trafficking experts. *Rolling Stone*. https://www.rollingstone.com/culture/culture-news/sound-of-freedom-child-trafficking-experts-1234786352/

Diffee, C. (2005). Sex and the city: The white slavery scare and social governance in the progressive era. *American Quarterly*, *57*(2), 411–437.

Ditmore, M. (2009). *The use of raids to fight trafficking in persons*. Sex Workers Project. chrome-extension://efaidnbmnnnibpcajpcglclefindmkaj/https://swp.urbanjustice.org/wp-content/uploads/sites/14/2019/09/swp-2009-raids-and-trafficking-report.pdf

Ditmore, M., & Thukral, J. (2012). Accountability and the use of raids to fight trafficking. *Anti-Trafficking Review*, *1*, 134–148.

DoCarmo, T. E. (2020). Ethical considerations for studying human trafficking. In J. Winterdyk & J. Jones (Eds.), *The Palgrave international handbook of human trafficking* (pp. 177–194). Springer International Publishing.

Doezema, J. (2000). Loose women or lost women? The re-emergence of the myth of white slavery in contemporary discourses of trafficking in women. *Gender Issues*, *18*(1), 23–50.

Doezema, J. (2002). Who gets to choose? Coercion, consent, and the UN trafficking protocol. *Gender and Development*, *10*(1), 20–27.

Doezema, J. (2010). *Sex slaves and discourse masters: The construction of trafficking*. Zed Books.

Doherty, Y. K., & Harris, A. (2015). The social construction of trafficked persons: An analysis of the UN protocol and the TVPA definitions. *Journal of Progressive Human Services*, *26*(1), 22–45.

Doychak, K., & Raghavan, C. (2020). "No voice or vote:" Trauma-coerced attachment in victims of sex trafficking. *Journal of Human Trafficking*, *6*(3), 339–357.

Eichert, D. (2019). It ruined my life: FOSTA, male escorts, and the construction of sexual victimhood in American politics. *Virginia Journal of Social Policy & the Law*, *26*(3), 201–245.

Ellison, G. (2017). Criminalizing the payment for sex in Northern Ireland: Sketching the contours of a moral panic. *The British Journal of Criminology*, *57*(1), 194–214.

Empower Foundation. (2012). *Hit and run: The impact of anti trafficking policy and practice on Sex Worker's Human Rights in Thailand*. The Empower Foundation. chrome-extension://efaidnbmnnnibpcajpcglclefindmkaj/http://www.empowerfoundation.org/sexy_file/Hit%20and%20Run%20%20RATSW%20Eng%20online.pdf

European Parliament. (2006). *Forced prostitution in the context of world sports events*. Resolution adopted March 15, 2006. https://www.europarl.europa.eu/doceo/document/TA-6-2006-0086_EN.html

Farr, K. (2004). *Sex trafficking: The global market in women and children*. Worth Publishers.

Farrell, A., Bright, K., de Vries, I., Pfeffer, R., & Dank, M. (2020). Policing labor trafficking in the United States. *Trends in Organized Crime*, *23*(1), 36–56.

Farrell, A., Dank, M., de Vries, I., Kafafian, M., Hughes, A., & Lockwood, S. (2019). Failing victims? Challenges of the police response to human trafficking. *Criminology & Public Policy*, *18*(3), 649–673.

Farrell, A., & Fahy, S. (2009). The problem of human trafficking in the U.S.: Public frames and policy responses. *Journal of Criminal Justice*, *37*(6), 617–626.

Farrell, A., McDevitt, J., Pfeffer, R., Fahy, S., Owens, C., Dank, M., & Adams, W. (2012). *Identifying challenges to improve the investigation and prosecution of state and local human trafficking cases: Executive summary*. National Institute of Justice. https://www.ojp.gov/ncjrs/virtual-library/abstracts/identifying-challenges-improve-investigation-and-prosecution-0

Farrell, A., Owens, C., & McDevitt, J. (2014). New laws but few cases: Understanding the challenges to the investigation and prosecution of human trafficking cases. *Crime, Law and Social Change*, *61*(2), 139–168.

Farrell, A., & Pfeffer, R. (2014). Policing human trafficking: Cultural blinders and organizational barriers. *The ANNALS of the American Academy of Political and Social Science*, *653*(1), 46–64.

Farrell, A., Pfeffer, R., & Bright, K. (2015). Police perceptions of human trafficking. *Journal of Crime and Justice*, *38*(3), 315–333.

Farrell, A., & Reichert, J. (2017). Using U.S. law-enforcement data: Promise and limits in measuring human trafficking. *Journal of Human Trafficking*, *3*(1), 39–60.

Fedina, L. (2015). Use and misuse of research in books on sex trafficking: Implications for interdisciplinary researchers, practitioners, and advocates. *Trauma, Violence, & Abuse*, *16*(2), 188–198.

Feehs, K., & Currier Wheeler, A. (2021). *2020 Federal Human Trafficking Report*. Human Trafficking Institute. https://www.traffickinginstitute.org/wp-content/uploads/2021/06/2020-Federal-Human-Trafficking-Report-Low-Res.pdf

Feingold, D. A. (2011). Trafficking in numbers: The social construction of human trafficking data. In P. Andreas & K. M. Greenhill (Eds.), *Sex, drugs, and body counts: The politics of numbers in global crime and conflict* (pp. 46–74). Cornell University Press.

Ferrell, J. (1999). Cultural criminology. *Annual Review of Sociology*, *2*, 395–418.

Ferrell, J. (2013). Cultural criminology and the politics of meaning. *Critical Criminology*, *21*(3), 257–271.

Ferrell, J., Hayward, K. J., & Young, J. (2015). *Cultural criminology*. SAGE Publications, Limited.

Finkel, R., & Finkel, M. L. (2015). The 'dirty downside' of global sporting events: Focus on human trafficking for sexual exploitation. *Public Health*, *129*(1), 17–22.

Francis, S., & Emser, M. (2014). *Media waves and moral panicking: The case of the FIFA World Cup 2010*. https://chesterrep.openrepository.com/handle/10034/621019

Funke, D. (2020, August 14). What's behind viral #SavetheChildren posts? Look to QAnon. *Tampa Bay Times*. https://www.tampabay.com/news/nation-world/2020/08/14/whats-behind-viral-savethechildren-posts-look-to-qanon/

GAATW. (2007). *Collateral damage: The impact of anti-trafficking measures on human rights around the world*. Global Alliance against Traffic in Women. https://gaatw.org/resources/publications/908-collateral-damage-the-impact-of-anti-trafficking-measures-on-human-rights-around-the-world

Gagnon, J. (2020). Rhetorical liminality in Southeast Asian media representations of human trafficking. In H. Park (Ed.), *Media culture in transnational Asia* (pp. 94–107). Rutgers University Press.

Gallagher, A., & Pearson, E. (2010). The high cost of freedom: A legal and policy analysis of shelter detention for victims of trafficking. *Human Rights Quarterly*, *32*(1), 73–114.

Gallagher, A. T. (2010). *The international law of human trafficking*. Cambridge University Press.

Gallagher, A. T. (2017). What's wrong with the global slavery index? *Anti-Trafficking Review*, *8*, 1–12.

Gans, H. J. (1980). *Deciding what's news: A study of CBS evening news, NBC nightly news, newsweek, and time*. Northwestern University Press.

GAO. (2006). *Human trafficking: Better data, strategy, and reporting needed to enhance U.S. antitrafficking efforts abroad.* https://www.gao.gov/products/gao-06-825

GAO. (2021). *Sex trafficking: Online platforms and federal prosecutions* (Report to Congressional Committees GAO-21-385). United States Government Accountability Office. chrome-extension://efaidnbmnnnibpcajpcglclefindmkaj/https://www.gao.gov/assets/gao-21-385.pdf

Garland, D. (2008). On the concept of moral panic. *Crime, Media, Culture*, *4*(1), 9–30.

Germany's World Cup Brothels: 40,000 Women and Children at Risk of Exploitation Through Trafficking: Hearing on 109–178 before the Subcommittee on Africa, Global Human Rights and International Operations of the Committee on International Relations, US House of Representatives Second. (2006). https://commdocs.house.gov/committees/intlrel/hfa27330.000/hfa27330_0.htm

Gezinski, L. B., & Gonzalez-Pons, K. M. (2022). Sex trafficking and technology: A systematic review of recruitment and exploitation. *Journal of Human Trafficking*, *0*(0), 1–15.

Gibbs, J. C., Strohacker, E. R., & Schally, J. L. (2023). Small and rural police chief perspectives on human trafficking in Pennsylvania. *Policing: An International Journal*, *46*(3), 521–534.

Goldenberg, A., Riggleman, D., Baumgartner, J., Marchl, L., Reid-Ross, A., Finkelstein, J., Hughes, B., Cain, C., Criezis, M., White, K., & Miller-Idriss, C. (2021). *The QAnon conspiracy: Destroying families, dividing communities, undermining democracy*. Network Contagion Research Institute. chrome-extension://efaidnbmnnnibpcajpcglclefindmkaj/https://networkcontagion.us/wp-content/uploads/NCRI-%E2%80%93-The-QAnon-Conspiracy-FINAL.pdf

Goode, E., & Ben-Yehuda, N. (1994). Moral panics: Culture, politics, and social construction. *Annual Review of Sociology*, *20*, 149–171.

Goode, E., & Ben-Yehuda, N. (2009). *Moral panics: The social construction of deviance*. Wiley.

Goodey, J. (2008). Human trafficking: Sketchy data and policy responses. *Criminology & Criminal Justice*, *8*(4), 421–442.

Gorham, D. (1978). The "maiden tribute of modern babylon" re-examined: Child prostitution and the idea of childhood in Late-Victorian England. *Victorian Studies*, *21*(3), 353–379.

Gould, C. (2010). Moral panic, human trafficking and the 2010 Soccer World Cup. *Agenda*, *24*(85), 31–44.

Goździak, E. M. (2015). Data matters: Issues and challenges for research on trafficking. In M. Dragiewicz (Ed.), *Global human trafficking: Critical issues and contexts* (pp. 23–37). Routledge.

Greenspan, R. E. (2020, July 13). How the wayfair human-trafficking conspiracy theory grew out of QAnon. *Business Insider*. https://www.insider.com/wayfair-human-trafficking-conspiracy-theory-tied-to-qanon-2020-7

Greer, C. (2010). News media criminology. In E. McLaughlin & T. Newburn (Eds.), *The SAGE handbook of criminological theory* (pp. 490–513). SAGE Publications Ltd.

Gregoriou, C., & Ras, I. A. (2018a). 'Call for purge on the people traffickers': An investigation into British newspapers' representation of transnational human trafficking, 2000–2016. In C. Gregoriou (Ed.), *Representations of transnational human trafficking: Present-day news media, true crime, and fiction* (pp. 25–60). Springer International Publishing.

Gregoriou, C., & Ras, I. A. (2018b). Representations of transnational human trafficking: A critical review. In C. Gregoriou (Ed.), *Representations of transnational human trafficking: Present-day news media, true crime, and fiction* (pp. 1–24). Springer International Publishing.

Gulati, J. (2010). *Media representation of human trafficking in the United States, Great Britain, and Canada* (SSRN Scholarly Paper 1633574).

Haag, P. (1999). *Consent: Sexual rights and the transformation of American liberalism.* Cornell University Press.

Hacker, D. (2015). Strategic compliance in the shadow of transnational anti-trafficking law. *Harvard Human Rights Journal, 28*(1), 11–64.

Hackett, J. (2022). Trafficking on film: A critical survey. In C. Murphy & R. Lazzarino (Eds.), *Modern slavery and human trafficking: The victim journey* (pp. 95–112). Policy Press.

Ham, J. (2011). *What's the cost of a rumour? A guide to sorting out the myths and the facts about sporting events and trafficking.* Global Alliance against Traffic in Women. https://gaatw.org/resources/publications/912-what-s-the-cost-of-a-rumour-a-guide-to-sorting-out-the-myths-and-the-facts-about-sporting-events-and-trafficking

Ham, J., Segrave, M., & Pickering, S. (2013). In the eyes of the beholder: Border enforcement, suspect travellers and trafficking victims. *Anti-Trafficking Review, 2*, Article 2.

Hayes, V. (2010). Human trafficking for sexual exploitation at world sporting events student notes. *Chicago-Kent Law Review, 85*(3), 1105–1146.

Haynes, D. F. (2014). The celebritization of human trafficking. *The ANNALS of the American Academy of Political and Social Science, 653*(1), 25–45.

Hayward, K. J. (2016). Cultural criminology: Script rewrites. *Theoretical Criminology, 20*(3), 297–321.

Hayward, K. J., & Young, J. (2004). Cultural criminology: Some notes on the script. *Theoretical Criminology, 8*(3), 259–273.

Heil, E., & Nichols, A. (2014). Hot spot trafficking: A theoretical discussion of the potential problems associated with targeted policing and the eradication of sex trafficking in the United States. *Contemporary Justice Review, 17*(4), 421–433.

Hennig, J., Craggs, S., Laczko, F., & Larsson, F. (2007). *Trafficking in human beings and the 2006 World Cup in Germany* (29; p. 54). IOM. https://www.iom.int/sites/g/files/tmzbdl486/files/2018-07/mrs29THBWCG.pdf

Herring, V. (2019, December 3). *Young warns of white vans abducting women, BPD confirms no reports.* WBAL. https://www.wbaltv.com/article/young-warns-of-white-vans-abducting-women/30101894

Heynen, R., & van der Meulen, E. (2022). Anti-trafficking saviors: Celebrity, slavery, and branded activism. *Crime, Media, Culture, 18*(2), 301–323.

Hill, A. (2016). How to stage a raid: Police, media and the master narrative of trafficking. *Anti- Trafficking Review, 7*, 1–8.

Hoang, K. K. (2016). Perverse humanitarianism and the business of rescue: What's wrong with NGOs and what's right about the "Johns"? In Ann Shola Orloff, Raka Ray, and Evren Savci., *Perverse politics? Feminism, anti- imperialism, multiplicity* (Vol. 30, pp. 19–43). Emerald Group Publishing Limited.

Hopper, E. K., & Gonzalez, L. D. (2018). A comparison of psychological symptoms in survivors of sex and labor trafficking. *Behavioral Medicine*, *44*(3), 177–188.

Hoyle, C., Bosworth, M., & Dempsey, M. (2011). Labelling the victims of sex trafficking: Exploring the borderland between rhetoric and reality. *Social & Legal Studies*, 20(3), 313-329.

Hua, J., & Nigorizawa, H. (2010). US sex trafficking, women's human rights and the politics of representation. *International Feminist Journal of Politics*, *12*(3–4), 401–423.

Huang, X., Yoder, B. R., Tsoukalas, A., Entress, R. M., & Sadiq, A.-A. (2022). Exploring the relationship between super bowls and potential online sex trafficking. *Trends in Organized Crime*, 1–23. https://doi.org/10.1007/s12117-022-09472-z

Hughes, D. M. (2000). The "Natasha" trade: The transnational shadow market of trafficking in women. *Journal of International Affairs; New York*, *53*(2), 625–651.

Hupp Williamson, S. (2017). Institutional anomie and socialist feminist theory: A process analysis of trafficking in post-socialist countries. In E. C. Heil & A. J. Nichols (Eds.), *Broadening the scope of human trafficking* (pp. 231–257). Carolina Academic Press.

Hupp Williamson, S. (2022). *Human trafficking in the era of global migration: Unravelling the impact of neoliberal economic policy*. Bristol University Press.

Hupp Williamson, S., Creel, S., & Walker, E. (2023). #WayfairGate and the growth of sex trafficking panics across social media. *Critical Criminology*, *31*(3), 617–633.

ILO. (2013). *Caught at sea: Forced labour and trafficking in fisheries*. International Labour Office. http://site.ebrary.com/id/10795029

International Convention for the Suppression of the Traffic in Women and Children, September 30, 1921, https://treaties.un.org/pages/ViewDetails.aspx?src=TREATY&mtdsg_no=VII-3&chapter=7&clang=_en

International Convention for the Suppression of the Traffic in Women of Full Age, October 11, 1933, https://treaties.un.org/pages/ViewDetails.aspx?src=TREATY&mtdsg_no=VII-5&chapter=7&clang=_en

Irwin, N. (2017). Police officer understandings of human trafficking and awareness of anti- trafficking measures. *Policing: An International Journal of Police Strategies & Management*, *40*(2), 291–305.

It's a Penalty. (2023). *Impact report super bowl LVII Arizona 2023*. It's a Penalty. https://itsapenalty.org/2023-arizona-campaign/

Jackson, C. A. (2016). Framing sex worker rights: How U.S. sex worker rights activists perceive and respond to mainstream anti–sex trafficking advocacy. *Sociological Perspectives*, *59*(1), 27–45.

Jac-Kucharski, A. (2012). The determinants of human trafficking: A US case study. *International Migration*, *50*(6), 150–165.

Jeffrey, L. A., & MacDonald, G. (2011). *Sex workers in the maritimes talk back*. UBC Press.

Jenkins, P. (2009). Failure to launch: Why do some social issues fail to detonate moral panics? *The British Journal of Criminology*, *49*(1), 35–47.

Jenkins, P., & Maier-Katkin, D. (1992). Satanism: Myth and reality in a contemporary moral panic. *Crime, Law and Social Change*, *17*(1), 53–76.

Jervis, R. (2011, January 31). Child sex rings spike during super bowl week. *USA Today*. http://www.usatoday.com/news/nation/2011-01-31-child-prostitution-super-bowl_N.htm

Johnston, A., Friedman, B., & Sobel, M. (2015). Framing an emerging issue: How U.S. print and broadcast news media covered sex trafficking, 2008–2012. *Journal of Human Trafficking, 1*(3), 235–254.

Jones, S., King, J., & Edwards, N. (2018). Human-trafficking prevention is not "sexy": Impact of the rescue industry on Thailand NGO programs and the need for a human rights approach. *Journal of Human Trafficking, 4*(3), 231–255.

Jones, T. R., & Kingshott, B. F. (2016). A feminist analysis of the American criminal justice system's response to human trafficking. *Criminal justice studies,* 29(3), 272-287.

Kakar, S. (2017). *Human trafficking.* Carolina Academic Press.

Kangaspunta, K., Sarrica, F., Johansen, R., Samson, J., Rybarska, A., & Whelan, K. (2018). *Global report on trafficking in persons 2018, booklet 2: Trafficking in persons in the context of armed conflict* (Global Report on Trafficking in Persons). UNODC. https://www.unodc.org/unodc/en/data-and-analysis/glotip-2018.html

Kaplan, A. (2021, June 2). *Here are the QAnon supporters running for Congress in 2022.* Media Matters for America. https://www.mediamatters.org/qanon-conspiracy-theory/here-are-qanon-supporters-running-congress-2022

Kara, S. (2010). *Sex trafficking: Inside the business of modern slavery.* Columbia University Press.

Kempadoo, K. (2001). Women of color and the global sex trade: Transnational feminist perspectives. *Meridians, 1*(2), 28–51.

Kempadoo, K. (2015). The modern-day white (wo)man's burden: Trends in anti-trafficking and anti-slavery campaigns. *Journal of Human Trafficking, 1*(1), 8–20.

Kenny, M. C., Helpingstine, C., & Borelus, T. (2023). Conspiracy theories of human trafficking: Knowledge and perceptions among a diverse college population. *Journal of Human Trafficking, 0*(0), 1–15.

Keo, C., Bouhours, T., Broadhurst, R., & Bouhours, B. (2014). Human trafficking and moral panic in Cambodia. *The Annals of the American Academy of Political and Social Science, 653*(1), 202–224.

Kessler, G. (2021, December 7). The fishy claim that '100,000 children' in the United States are in the sex trade. *Washington Post.* https://www.washingtonpost.com/news/fact-checker/wp/2015/09/02/the-fishy-claim-that-100000-children-in-the-united-states-are-in-the-sex-trade/

Kligman, G., & Limoncelli, S. (2005). Trafficking women after socialism: From, to, and through Eastern Europe. *Social Politics: International Studies in Gender, State and Society, 12*(1), 118–140.

Klobuchar, A. (2014, January 17). *Klobuchar, Cindy McCain meet with NFL to discuss efforts to Crack Down on sex trafficking Ahead of super bowl.* U.S. Senator Amy Klobuchar. https://www.klobuchar.senate.gov/public/index.cfm/2014/1/klobuchar-cindy-mccain-meet-with-nfl-to-discuss-efforts-to-crack-down-on-sex-trafficking-ahead-of-super-bowl

Klocke, B. V., & Muschert, G. W. (2010). A hybrid model of moral panics: Synthesizing the theory and practice of moral panic research. *Sociology Compass, 4*(5), 295–309.

Kraft, A. (2020, August 21). Conspiracy theories surrounding human trafficking is taking a toll on survivor resources. *WNCT.* https://www.wnct.com/news/conspiracy-theories-surrounding-human-trafficking-is-taking-a-toll-on-survivor-resources/?utm_source=pocket_reader

Kranrattanasuit, N. (2014). *ASEAN and human trafficking: Case studies of Cambodia, Thailand and Vietnam*. Brill Nijhoff.

Laczko, F., & Gramegna, M. A. (2003). Developing better indicators of human trafficking. *The Brown Journal of World Affairs*, *10*(1), 179–194.

Lagler, A. R. (2000). *"For god's sake do something": White -slavery narratives and moral panic in turn -of -the -century American cities*. Ph.D., Michigan State University.

Lammasniemi, L. (2020). International legislation on white slavery and anti-trafficking in the early twentieth century. In J. Winterdyk & J. Jones (Eds.), *The Palgrave international handbook of human trafficking* (pp. 67–78). Springer International Publishing.

Le, L., & Wyndham, C. (2022). What we know about human traffickers in Vietnam. *Anti-trafficking Review*, (18), 33-48.

Lee, M. (2011). *Trafficking and global crime control*. SAGE.

Lee, M. (2014). Gendered discipline and protective custody of trafficking victims in Asia. *Punishment & Society*, *16*(2), 206–222.

Lepp, A. (2013). Repeat performance? Human trafficking and the 2010 Vancouver Winter Olympic Games. In E. V. der Meulen, E. M. Durisin, & V. Love (Eds.), *Selling sex: Experience, advocacy, and research on sex work in Canada* (p. 251). UBC Press.

Limoncelli, S. (2010). *The politics of trafficking: The first international movement to combat the sexual exploitation of women*. Stanford University Press.

Limoncelli, S. A. (2009a). Human trafficking: Globalization, exploitation, and transnational sociology. *Sociology Compass*, *3*(1), 72–91.

Limoncelli, S. A. (2009b). The trouble with trafficking: Conceptualizing women's sexual labor and economic human rights. *Women's Studies International Forum*, *32*(4), 261–269.

Lindgren, S. (2005). Social constructionism and criminology: Traditions, problems and possibilities. *Journal of Scandinavian Studies in Criminology & Crime Prevention*, *6*(1), 4–22.

Litam, S. D. A., Oh, S., & Conrad, M. J. (2023). Human trafficking myths as a mediator in the relationship between ambivalent sexism and sex trafficking attitudes among undergraduate, medical, and public health students. *Journal of Human Trafficking*, *0*(0), 1–17.

Lourenço, E., Gonçalves, M., & Matos, M. (2019). Trafficking in human beings: Portuguese magistrates' perceptions. *Journal of Human Trafficking*, *5*(3), 238–254.

Lutnick, A. (2016). Domestic minor sex trafficking: Beyond victims and villains. In *Domestic minor sex trafficking*. Columbia University Press.

Mahdavi, P. (2011). *Gridlock: Labor, migration, and human trafficking in Dubai*. Stanford University Press.

Maher, L., Dixon, T. C., Phlong, P., Mooney-Somers, J., Stein, E. S., & Page, K. (2015). Conflicting rights: How the prohibition of human trafficking and sexual exploitation infringes the right to health of female sex workers in Phnom Penh, Cambodia. *Health and Human Rights*, *17*(1), 102–113.

Mai, N. (2013). Embodied cosmopolitanisms: The subjective mobility of migrants working in the global sex industry. *Gender, Place & Culture*, *20*(1), 107–124.

Majic, P. S. (2023). *Lights, camera, feminism? Celebrities and anti-trafficking politics*. University of California Press.

Majic, S. (2020). Same same but different? Gender, sex work, and respectability politics in the MyRedBook and Rentboy closures. *Anti-Trafficking Review*, *14*, 82–98.

Majic, S. A. (2018). Real men set norms? Anti-trafficking campaigns and the limits of celebrity norm entrepreneurship. *Crime, Media, Culture*, *14*(2), 289–309.

Malarek, V. (2011). *The Natashas: The new global sex trade*. Penguin Canada.

Mapp, S., Hornung, E., D'Almeida, M., & Juhnke, J. (2016). Local law enforcement officers' knowledge of human trafficking: Ability to define, identify, and assist. *Journal of Human Trafficking*, *2*(4), 329–342.

Marchionni, D. M. (2012). International human trafficking: An agenda-building analysis of the US and British press. *International Communication Gazette*, *74*(2), 145–158.

Marcus, A., Horning, A., Curtis, R., Sanson, J., & Thompson, E. (2014). Conflict and agency among sex workers and pimps: A closer look at domestic minor sex trafficking. *The ANNALS of the American Academy of Political and Social Science*, *653*(1), 225–246.

Martin, L., & Hill, A. (2017). *Sex trafficking and the 2018 super bowl in Minneapolis: A research brief* [Report]. http://conservancy.umn.edu/handle/11299/226835

Martin, L., & Hill, A. (2019). Debunking the myth of 'super bowl sex trafficking': Media hype or evidenced-based coverage. *Anti-Trafficking Review*, *13*, 13–29.

Matheson, C. M., & Finkel, R. (2013). Sex trafficking and the Vancouver Winter Olympic Games: Perceptions and preventative measures. *Tourism Management*, *36*, 613–628.

Mathias, C. (2023, October 27). *What 'Woodhull' won't change: Five years of chilling effects under FOSTA*. Center for Democracy and Technology. https://cdt.org/insights/what-woodhull-wont-change-five-years-of-chilling-effects-under-fosta/

Matsueda, R. L. (2014). The natural history of labeling theory. In D. P. Farrington & J. Murray (Eds.), *Labeling theory: Empirical tests* (pp. 13–44). Taylor & Francis Group.

McNeal, S. (2020, July 14). The conspiracy theory about wayfair is spreading quickly among lifestyle influencers on Instagram. *BuzzFeed News*. https://www.buzzfeednews.com/article/stephaniemcneal/wayfair-qanon-influencers-instagram

McNeill, M. (2021, October 26). Lies, damned lies and sex work statistics. *Washington Post*. https://www.washingtonpost.com/news/the-watch/wp/2014/03/27/lies-damned-lies-and-sex-work-statistics/

McRobbie, A., & Thornton, S. L. (1995). Rethinking "moral panic" for multi-mediated social worlds. *The British Journal of Sociology*, *46*(4), 559–574.

Mendel, J., & Sharapov, K. (2016). Human trafficking and online networks: Policy, analysis, and ignorance. *Antipode*, *48*(3), 665–684.

Merlan, A. (2023, August 7). Trafficking survivors and advocates are being harassed by 'sound of freedom' fans. *Vice*. https://www.vice.com/en/article/epvbyz/trafficking-survivors-and-advocates-are-being-harassed-by-sound-of-freedom-fans

Merry, S. E. (2016). *The seductions of quantification: Measuring human rights, gender violence, and sex trafficking*. The University of Chicago Press.

Milivojevic, S., Moore, H., & Segrave, M. (2020). Freeing the modern slaves, one click at a time: Theorising human trafficking, modern slavery, and technology. *Anti-Trafficking Review*, *14*, 16–32.

Milivojević, S., & Pickering, S. (2008). Football and sex: The 2006 FIFA World Cup and sex trafficking. *Temida*, *11*(2), 21–47.

Miller, K., Kennedy, E., & Dubrawski, A. (2016). Do public events affect sex trafficking activity? *arXiv:1602.05048 [Stat]*. http://arxiv.org/abs/1602.05048

Mishra, V. (2015). *Combating human trafficking: Gaps in policy and law*. SAGE.

Mitchell, G. (2016). Evangelical Ecstasy meets Feminist Fury: Sex trafficking, moral panics, and homonationalism during global sporting events. *GLQ: A Journal of Lesbian and Gay Studies*, *22*(3), 325–357.

Mitchell, G. (2022). *Panics without borders: How global sporting events drive myths about sex trafficking*. University of California Press.

Mobasher, Z., Baldwin, S. B., Navarro, B., Bressler-Montgomery, D., King, J., Family, L., Smith, L. V., & Kuo, T. (2022). Knowledge and perceptions of human trafficking among community-based and faith-based organization members in South Los Angeles. *Global Health Promotion*, *29*(3), 45–56.

Moran, R. E., & Prochaska, S. (2023). Misinformation or activism? Analyzing networked moral panic through an exploration of #SaveTheChildren. *Information, Communication & Society*, *26*(16), 3197–3217.

Moran, R. E., Prochaska, S., Grasso, I., & Schlegel, I. (2023). Navigating information-seeking in conspiratorial waters: Anti-trafficking advocacy and education post QAnon. *Proceedings of the ACM on Human-Computer Interaction*, *7*(CSCW1), 77:1–77:27.

Morero, M. (2022). Police perceptions of human trafficking in South Africa miscellaneous. *Technium Social Sciences Journal*, *27*, 824–836.

Morgan, J. (2006, May 24). Methodist' fears over World Cup brothels. *Whitehaven News*. https://www.whitehavennews.co.uk/news/17173946.methodist-fears-over-world-cup-brothels/

Murthy, D. (2012). Towards a sociological understanding of social media: Theorizing Twitter. *Sociology*, *46*(6), 1059–1073.

Musto, J. (2016). *Control and protect: Collaboration, carceral protection, and domestic sex trafficking in the United States*. University of California Press.

Musto, J., Fehrenbacher, A. E., Hoefinger, H., Mai, N., Macioti, P. G., Bennachie, C., Giametta, C., & D'Adamo, K. (2021). Anti-trafficking in the time of FOSTA/SESTA: Networked moral gentrification and sexual humanitarian creep. *Social Sciences*, *10*(58), Article 1–18.

Musto, J. L. (2009). What's in a name? Conflations and contradictions in contemporary U.S. discourses of human trafficking. *Women's Studies International Forum*, *32*(4), 281–287.

Musto, J. L., & boyd, d. (2014). The trafficking-technology nexus. *Social Politics: International Studies in Gender, State & Society*, *21*(3), 461–483.

Muždeka, N. (2018). Not all human trafficking is created equal: Transnational human trafficking in the UK and Serbian News Media texts—narratological and media studies approaches. In C. Gregoriou (Ed.), *Representations of transnational human trafficking: Present-day news media, true crime, and fiction* (pp. 61–88). Springer International Publishing.

Muzzatti, S. L., & Smith, E. M. (2018). Cultural criminology. In W. S. DeKeseredy & M. Dragiewicz (Eds.), *Routledge handbook of critical criminology* (2nd ed., pp. 107–119). Routledge.

NCMEC. (2022). *Missing children statistics*. https://www.missingkids.org/ourwork/impact

Nichols, A. J. (2016). *Sex trafficking in the United States: Theory, research, policy, and practice*. Columbia University Press.

Nichols, A. J. (2016). Global inequality and human trafficking: The organ and tissue trade. In E. C. Heil & A. J. Nichols (Eds.), *Broadening the scope of human trafficking* (pp. 25–41). Carolina Academic Press.

Nichols, A. J., & Heil, E. C. (2015). Challenges to identifying and prosecuting sex trafficking cases in the Midwest United States. *Feminist Criminology*, *10*(1), 7–35.

North, A. (2020, September 18). #SaveTheChildren is pulling American moms into QAnon— Vox. *Vox*. https://www.vox.com/21436671/save-our-children-hashtag-qanon-pizzagate

O'Brien, E. (2013). Ideal victims in human trafficking awareness campaigns. In K. Carrington, M. Ball, E. O'Brien, & J. M. Tauri (Eds.), *Crime, justice and social democracy* (pp. 315–326). Palgrave Macmillan.

O'Brien, E. (2016). Human trafficking heroes and villains: Representing the problem in anti- trafficking awareness campaigns. *Social & Legal Studies*, *25*(2), 205–224.

O'Brien, E., & McLeod, S. (2011). Vulnerable and invisible: Depictions of trafficking victims in public awareness campaigns. In R. Walters & K. Carrington (Eds.), *Crime, justice and social democracy conference proceedings 2011* (pp. 43–60). Queensland University of Technology. http://www.crimejusticeconference.com/

Outshoorn, J. (2005). The political debates on prostitution and trafficking of women. *Social Politics: International Studies in Gender, State and Society*, *12*(1), 141–155.

Outshoorn, J. (2015). The trafficking policy debates. In M. Dragiewicz (Ed.), *Global human trafficking [electronic resource]: Critical issues and contexts* (pp. 7–22). Routledge.

Owens, C., Dank, M., Farrell, A., Breaux, J., Banuelos, I., Pfeffer, R., Heitsmith, R., Bright, K., & McDevitt, J. (2014). *Understanding the organization, operation, and victimization process of labor trafficking in the United States*. The Urban Institute. https://www.urban.org/research/publication/understanding-organization-operation-and-victimization-process-labor-trafficking-united-states/view/full_report

Page, M., & Worden, M. (2022, November 30). *Qatar World Cup chief publicly admits high migrant death tolls*. Human Rights Watch. https://www.hrw.org/news/2022/11/30/qatar-world-cup-chief-publicly-admits-high-migrant-death-tolls

Pajnik, M. (2010). Media framing of trafficking. *International Feminist Journal of Politics*, *12*(1), 45–64.

People Staff. (2011, February 7). Demi Moore's valentine's day gift that gives back. *People Magazine*. https://people.com/style/demi-moores-valentines-day-gift-that-gives-back/

Peters, A. W. (2013). "Things that involve sex are just different": US anti-trafficking law and policy on the books, in their minds, and in action. *Anthropological Quarterly*, *86*(1), 221–255.

Petrunov, G. (2014). Human trafficking in Eastern Europe: The case of Bulgaria. *The Annals of the American Academy of Political and Social Science*, *653*(1), 162–182.

Piquero, A. R., Piquero, N. L., & Riddell, J. R. (2021). Do (sex) crimes increase during the United States Formula 1 Grand Prix? *Journal of Experimental Criminology*, *17*(1), 87–108.

Play Fair. (2007). *No medal for the Olympics on labour rights*. Play Fair Campaign. https://hdl.handle.net/1813/100288

Pliley, J. R. (2019). Trafficked white slaves and misleading marriages in the campaigns against sex trafficking, 1885–1927. *Federal History*, *11*, 60–82.

Polaris. (2017). *The typology of modern slavery: Defining sex and labor trafficking in the United States*. Polaris Project. https://polarisproject.org/resources/the-typology-of-modern-slavery-defining-sex-and-labor-trafficking-in-the-united-states/

Polaris. (2019). *Human trafficking at home: Labor trafficking of domestic workers*. Polaris Project. https://polarisproject.org/resources/human-trafficking-at-home-labor-trafficking-of-domestic-workers/

Polaris. (2020, July 20). *Polaris statement on wayfair sex trafficking claims*. Polaris Project. https://polarisproject.org/press-releases/polaris-statement-on-wayfair-sex-trafficking-claims/

Polaris. (2021a). *Labor trafficking on specific temporary work visas report*. Polaris Project. https://polarisproject.org/resources/labor-trafficking-on-specific-temporary-work-visas-report/

Polaris. (2021b). *Recruitment, human trafficking, and temporary visa workers*. Polaris Project. https://polarisproject.org/resources/recruitment-human-trafficking-and-temporary-visa-workers/

Polaris Project. (2020, September 25). *Human trafficking rumors*. https://polarisproject.org/human-trafficking-rumors/

Prakash, J., Erickson, T. B., & Stoklosa, H. (2022). Human trafficking and the growing malady of disinformation. *Frontiers in Public Health, 10,* 1–5.

Preble, K. M., Basham, R. E., Mengo, C., & Richards, T. (2016). Human trafficking: An exploratory review of awareness and training videos. *Journal of Human Trafficking, 2*(3), 221–234.

Presdee, M. (2004). Cultural criminology: The long and winding road. *Theoretical Criminology, 8*(3), 275–285.

Raby, K., & Chazal, N. (2022). The Myth of the 'Ideal Offender': Challenging persistent human trafficking stereotypes through emerging Australian cases. *Anti-trafficking Review*, (18), 13-32.

Rafter, N. H. (1990). The social construction of crime and crime control. *Journal of Research in Crime and Delinquency, 27*(4), 376–389.

Rajan, A., Chen, C., Benjamin, C., Saltskog, M., Blazakis, J., Schwitzky, Z., & McClintock, L. (2021). *Countering QAnon: Understanding the role of human trafficking in the disinformation-extremist nexus*. Polaris. https://polarisproject.org/resources/countering-qanon-understanding-the-role-of-human-trafficking-in-the-disinformation-extremist-nexus/

Reis, T. A., Gibbs, J. C., Howard, D., & Strohacker, E. R. (2022). Prostitute or human trafficking victim? Police discernment of human trafficking. *Policing: An International Journal, 45*(2), 334–345.

Richardson, S. (2008). *"One year of my blood": Exploitation of migrant construction workers in Beijing*. Human Rights Watch. https://www.hrw.org/report/2008/03/11/one-year-my-blood/exploitation-migrant-construction-workers-beijing

Richter, M., & Delva, W. (2011). *"Maybe it will be better once this World Cup has passed": Research findings regarding the impact of the 2010 Soccer World Cup on sex work in South Africa*. United Nation Population Fund. http://www.migration.org.za/wp-content/uploads/2017/08/%E2%80%9CMaybe-it-will-be-better-once-this-World-Cup-has-passed%E2%80%9D.pdf

Richter, M., Luchters, S., Ndlovu, D., Temmerman, M., & Chersich, M. F. (2012). Female sex work and international sport events – no major changes in demand or supply of paid sex during the 2010 Soccer World Cup: A cross-sectional study. *BMC Public Health, 12*(1), 763.

Ritzer, G. (2010). *Globalization: A basic text.* Wiley-Blackwell.

Roche, M. (2000). *Megaevents and modernity: Olympics and expos in the growth of global culture*. Routledge.

Rodríguez-López, S. (2018). (De)constructing stereotypes: Media representations, social perceptions, and legal responses to human trafficking. *Journal of Human Trafficking, 4*(1), 61–72.

Roe-Sepowitz, D., Gallagher, J., Bracy, K., Cantelme, L., Bayless, A., Larkin, J., Reese, A., & Allbee, L. (2015). *Exploring the impact of the super bowl on sex trafficking 2015*. The McCain Institute for International Leadership. https://www.scribd.com/doc/256655029/Exploring-the-Impact-of-the-Super-Bowl-on-Sex-Trafficking-2015

Rogers, K. (2020, October 15). Trump Said QAnon 'fights' Pedophilia. But the group has made it harder to protect kids. *FiveThirtyEight*. https://fivethirtyeight.com/features/qanons-obsession-with-savethechildren-is-making-it-harder-to-save-kids-from-traffickers/

Rohloff, A., Hughes, J., Petley, J., & Critcher, C. (2013). Moral panics in the contemporary world: Enduring controversies and future directions. In J. Petley, C. Critcher, J. Hughes, & A. Rohloff (Eds.), *Moral panics in the contemporary world* (pp. 1–29). Bloomsbury Publishing USA.

Rohloff, A., & Wright, S. (2010). Moral panic and social theory: Beyond the heuristic. *Current Sociology, 58*(3), 403–419.

Roose, K. (2020, September 28). How 'save the children' is keeping QAnon alive. *The New York Times*. https://www.nytimes.com/2020/09/28/technology/save-the-children-qanon.html

Roots, K. (2020). Human trafficking in Canada as a historical continuation of the 1980s and 1990s panics over youth in sex trade. In J. Winterdyk & J. Jones (Eds.), *The Palgrave international handbook of human Trafficking* (pp. 97–113). Springer International Publishing.

Rothman, E. F., Farrell, A., Bright, K., & Paruk, J. (2018). Ethical and practical considerations for collecting research-related data from commercially sexually exploited children. *Behavioral Medicine, 44*(3), 250–258.

Russell, A. (2018). Human trafficking: A research synthesis on human-trafficking literature in academic journals from 2000–2014. *Journal of Human Trafficking, 4*(2), 114–136.

Salami, T., Babu, J., & Hari, C. (2022). Criminal justice students' perceptions of human trafficking victims: Assessing bias and helping behavior. *Journal of Criminal Justice Education, 33*(1), 93–109.

Sanchez, R. V., Speck, P. M., & Patrician, P. A. (2019). A concept analysis of trauma coercive bonding in the commercial sexual exploitation of children. *Journal of Pediatric Nursing, 46*, 48–54.

Sanford, R., Martínez, D. E., & Weitzer, R. (2016). Framing human trafficking: A content analysis of recent U.S. newspaper articles. *Journal of Human Trafficking, 2*(2), 139–155.

Sant, S.-L., Maleske, C., Wang, W., & King, E. J. (2023). Leveraging sport events for the promotion of human rights in host communities: Diffusion of anti-trafficking campaigns at Super Bowl LIV. *Sport Management Review, 26*(2), 203–223.

Sarkar, S. (2015). Use of technology in human trafficking networks and sexual exploitation: A cross-sectional multi-country study. *Transnational Social Review, 5*(1), 55–68.

Sassen, S. (2002). Women's burden: Counter-geographies of globalization and the feminization of survival. *Nordic Journal of International Law, 71*(2), 255–274.

Saunders, P., & Soderlund, G. (2003). Threat or opportunity? Sexuality, gender and the ebb and flow of trafficking as discourse. *Canadian Woman Studies/Les Cahiers de La Femme, 22*(3/4), 16–24.

Savona, E. U., & Stefanizzi, S. (2007). *Measuring human trafficking: Complexities and pitfalls*. Springer Science & Business Media.

Scarpa, S. (2020). UN Palermo trafficking protocol eighteen years On: A critique. In J. Winterdyk & J. Jones (Eds.), *The Palgrave international handbook of human trafficking* (pp. 623–640). Springer International Publishing.

Seitz, A., & Swenson, A. (2020, July 16). Baseless wayfair child-trafficking theory spreads online. *AP News*. https://apnews.com/article/social-media-us-news-ap-top-news-conspiracy-media-9d54570ebba5e406667c38cb29522ec6

Sharapov, K. (2019). Public understanding of trafficking in human beings in Great Britain, Hungary and Ukraine. *Anti-Trafficking Review, 13*, 30–49.

Sharma, N. (2005). Anti-trafficking rhetoric and the making of a global apartheid. *NWSA Journal, 17*(3), 88–111.

Shelley, L. I. (2010). *Human trafficking: A global perspective*. Cambridge University Press.

Shih, E. (2016). Not in my "backyard abolitionism": Vigilante rescue against American sex trafficking. *Sociological Perspectives, 59*(1), 66–90.

Skilbrei, M.-L., & Tveit, M. (2008). Defining trafficking through empirical work: Blurred boundaries and their consequences. *Gender, Technology and Development, 12*(1), 9–30.

Small, J. L. (2012). Trafficking in truth: Media, sexuality, and human rights evidence. *Feminist Studies, 38*(2), 415–443.

Snow, O. (2022, December 26). Sex workers have been banned from airbnb for years. Will you be next? *The Nation*. https://www.thenation.com/article/society/airbnb-banning-sex-workers/

Sobel, M. R. (2014). Chronicling a crisis: Media framing of human trafficking in India, Thailand, and the USA. *Asian Journal of Communication, 24*(4), 315–332.

Sobel, M. R. (2016). Confronting sex trafficking: Gender depictions in newspaper coverage from the former Soviet Republics and the Baltic states. *European Journal of Communication, 31*(2), 152–168.

Soderlund, G. (2002). Covering urban vice: The New York Times, "white slavery," and the construction of journalistic knowledge. *Critical Studies in Media Communication, 19*(4), 438–460.

Soderlund, G. (2005). Running from the rescuers: New U.S. Crusades against sex trafficking and the rhetoric of abolition. *NWSA Journal, 17*(3), 64–87.

South African Police Service. (2011). *Crime statistics report 2010/2011*. South African Police Service. chrome-extension://efaidnbmnnnibpcajpcglclefindmkaj/https://www.gov.za/sites/default/files/gcis_document/201409/sapscrimereprt0.pdf

Spector, M., & Kitsuse, J. I. (1973). Social problems: A re-formulation. *Social Problems, 21*(2), 145–159.

Srikantiah, J. (2007). Perfect victims and real survivors: The iconic victim in domestic human trafficking law. *Immigration and Nationality Law Review*, *28*, 741–798.

Steele, S. L., & Shores, T. (2014). More than just a famous face: Exploring the rise of the celebrity expert-advocate through anti-trafficking action by the Demi and Ashton Foundation. *Crime, Media, Culture*, *10*(3), 259–272.

Stickle, W., Hickman, S., & White, C. (2020). *Human trafficking: A comprehensive exploration of modern day slavery*. SAGE Publications.

Stiles, S. (2018). Good versus evil or "saying more": Strategies of telling in sex trafficking documentary films. *Journal of Human Trafficking*, *4*(1), 35–47.

Stone, M. (2005). Twenty-first century global sex trafficking: Migration, capitalism, class, and challenges for feminism now. *English Studies in Canada; Edmonton*, *31*(2/3), 31–38.

Strohacker, E., Gibbs, J. C., & Woolford, S. (2023). Pennsylvanians' perceptions of the Nature and Extent of human trafficking. *Journal of Human Trafficking*, *9*(2), 212–228.

Surtees, R. (2008). Traffickers and trafficking in Southern and Eastern Europe: Considering the other side of human trafficking. *European Journal of Criminology*, *5*(1), 39–68.

SWAN, & GHJP. (2020). *Sex work vs trafficking: How they are different and why it matters*. Sex Workers Alliance Network and Yale Global Health Justice Partnership. https://law.yale.edu/sites/default/files/area/center/ghjp/documents/issue_brief_sex_work_ vs_trafficking_v2.pdf

Szablewska, N., & Kubacki, K. (2018). Anti-human trafficking campaigns: A systematic literature review. *Social Marketing Quarterly*, *24*(2), 104–122.

Szörényi, A., & Eate, P. (2014). Saving virgins, saving the USA: Heteronormative masculinities and the securitisation of trafficking discourse in mainstream narrative film. *Social Semiotics*, *24*(5), 608–622.

Talbot, A., & Carter, T. F. (2018). Human rights abuses at the Rio 2016 Olympics: Activism and the media. *Leisure Studies*, *37*(1), 77–88.

The Dangers of A Large City, or The System of The Underworld: Exposing The White Slave Traffic,. Max Stein Publishing, Chicago.. (1900).

Thomas, W. I., & Thomas, D. S. (1928). *The child in America*. Knopf.

Tiffany, K. (2021, December 9). *The great (fake) child-sex-trafficking epidemic*. The Atlantic. https://www.theatlantic.com/magazine/archive/2022/01/children-sex-trafficking-conspiracy-epidemic/620845/

Tillyer, M. S., Smith, M. R., & Tillyer, R. (2023). Findings from the U.S. National Human Trafficking Hotline. *Journal of Human Trafficking*, *9*(3), 398–407.

TIP. (2012). *Trafficking in Persons report 2012*. U.S. Department of State. https://www.state.gov/documents/organization/192594.pdf

TIP. (2015). *Trafficking in Persons report*. US State Department. https://2009-2017.state.gov/j/tip/rls/tiprpt/2015/index.htm

Todres, J. (2009). Law, otherness, and human trafficking. *Santa Clara Law Review*, *49*(3), 605–672.

Todres, J. (2016). Human trafficking and film: How popular portrayals influence law and public perception. *Cornell Law Review Online*, *101*, 1–24.

Tosh, S. (2019). Drugs, crime, and aggravated felony deportations: Moral panic theory and the legal construction of the "criminal alien." *Critical Criminology*, *27*(2), 329–345.

Triplett, R., & Upton, L. (2015). Labeling theory: Past, present, and future. In A. R. Piquero & M. L. Rorie (Eds.), *The handbook of criminological theory* (pp. 297–315). John Wiley & Sons, Incorporated.

Tripp, T. M., & McMahon-Howard, J. (2016). Perception vs. reality: The relationship between organized crime and human trafficking in Metropolitan Atlanta. *American Journal of Criminal Justice*, *41*(4), 732–764.

Truong, T.-D. (2003). Gender, exploitative migration, and the sex industry: A European perspective. *Gender, Technology and Development*, *7*(1), 31–52.

Twis, M. K. (2020). Predicting different types of victim-trafficker relationships: A multinomial logistic regression analysis. *Journal of Human Trafficking*, *6*(4), 450–466.

Tyldum, G. (2010). Limitations in research on human trafficking*. *International Migration*, *48*(5), 1–13.

Tyldum, G., & Brunovskis, A. (2005). Describing the unobserved: Methodological challenges in empirical studies on human trafficking. *International Migration*, *43*(1/2), 17–34.

Ugwudike, P. (2015). *An introduction to critical criminology*. Policy Press.

University of Maryland. (2023, December 11). *QAnon Crime Maps*. National Consortium for the Study of Terrorism and Responses to Terrorism. https://www.start.umd.edu/qanon-crime-maps

United States Trafficking Victims Protection Act, October 28, 2000, https://www.justice.gov/humantrafficking/key-legislation

United Nations Protocol to Prevent, Suppress and Punish Trafficking in Persons, Especially Women and Children, November 15, 2000, https://www.ohchr.org/en/instruments-mechanisms/instruments/protocol-prevent-suppress-and-punish-trafficking-persons

UNODC. (2020). *Global report on trafficking in persons*. United Nations Office of Drugs and Crime. https://www.unodc.org/unodc/data-and-analysis/glotip.html

Urban, L. S., & Arends, V. (2018). The (in)frequency of organized crime involvement: Human trafficking in Missouri. *Journal of Gang Research*, *25*(4), 23–43.

U.S. DOJ. (2003). *Assessment of U.S. activities to combat trafficking in persons*. US Department of Justice. https://2001-2009.state.gov/g/tip/rls/rpt/23495.htm

Uscinski, J. E., & Enders, A. (2021, March 9). Unfounded fears about sex trafficking did not begin with QAnon and go far beyond it. *USApp – American Politics and Policy Blog*. https://blogs.lse.ac.uk/usappblog/

Uscinski, J. E., & Enders, A. M. (2023). What is a conspiracy theory and why does it matter? *Critical Review*, *35*(1–2), 148–169.

Vermeulen, G., Damme, Y. V., & Bondt, W. D. (2010). Perceived involvement of "organised crime" in human trafficking and smuggling. *Revue internationale de droit penal*, *81*(1), 247–273.

Viuhko, M. (2018). Hardened professional criminals, or just friends and relatives? The diversity of offenders in human trafficking. *International Journal of Comparative and Applied Criminal Justice*, 42(2-3), 177-193.

Vocks, J., & Nijboer, J. (2000). The promised land: A study of trafficking in women from Central and Eastern Europe to the Netherlands. *European Journal on Criminal Policy and Research*, *8*(3), 379–388.

Wallace, K. (2010, February 2). Human trafficking alive and well for the 2010 Olympics. *The Vancouver Observer*. https://www.vancouverobserver.com/politics/commentary/2010/02/02/human-trafficking-alive-and-well-2010-olympics.html

Watson, S. D. (2023). Conspiracy theories and human trafficking: Coercive power, normative ambiguity and epistemic uncertainty. *Journal of Human Trafficking, 0*(0), 1–18.

Weitzer, R. (2007). The social construction of sex trafficking: Ideology and institutionalization of a moral crusade. *Politics & Society, 35*(3), 447–475.

Weitzer, R. (2014). New directions in research on human trafficking. *The ANNALS of the American Academy of Political and Social Science, 653*(1), 6–24.

Weitzer, R. (2015). Human trafficking and contemporary slavery. *Annual Review of Sociology, 41*(1), 223–242.

Weitzer, R. (2020). The campaign against sex work in the United States: A successful moral crusade. *Sexuality Research and Social Policy, 17*(3), 399–414.

Whitney, J., Jennex, M., Elkins, A., & Frost, E. (2018, January 3). *Don't want to get caught? Don't say It: The use of EMOJIS in online human sex trafficking ads.* Proceedings of the 51st Hawaii International Conference on System Sciences, Waikoloa Village, HI. http://hdl.handle.net/10125/50426

Wilson, D. G., Walsh, W. F., & Kleuber, S. (2006). Trafficking in human beings: Training and services among US law enforcement agencies. *Police Practice and Research, 7*(2), 149–160.

Wilson, M., & O'Brien, E. (2016). Constructing the ideal victim in the United States of America's annual trafficking in persons reports. *Crime, Law and Social Change, 65*(1–2), 29–45.

Worden, M. (2015). *Raising the Bar: Mega-Sporting Events and Human Rights*. Human Rights Watch. https://www.hrw.org/world-report/2015/country-chapters/global-1

Young, J. (1971). *The Drugtakers: The Social Meaning of Drug Use*. MacGibbon & Kee.

Zhang, S. (2007). *Smuggling and trafficking in human beings: All roads lead to America*. Praeger Publishers.

Zhang, S. (2009). Beyond the 'Natasha' story – a review and critique of current research on sex trafficking. *Global Crime, 10*(3), 178–195.

Zhang, S. (2010). *Sex trafficking in a border community: A field study of sex trafficking in Tijuana, Mexico*. National Institute of Justice.

Zhang, S. (2012). Measuring labor trafficking: A research note. *Crime, Law and Social Change, 85*(4), 469–482.

Zhang, S., Spiller, M. W., Finch, B. K., & Yang, Q. (2014). Estimating labor trafficking among unauthorized migrant workers in San Diego. *The ANNALS of the American Academy of Political and Social Science, 653*(1), 65–86.

Index

For Product Safety Concerns and Information please contact our EU representative GPSR@taylorandfrancis.com
Taylor & Francis Verlag GmbH, Kaufingerstraße 24, 80331 München, Germany

www.ingramcontent.com/pod-product-compliance
Lightning Source LLC
LaVergne TN
LVHW010931110826
845149LV00013B/2543

* 9 7 8 1 0 3 2 5 7 3 5 7 1 *